IN THE SHADOW OF LOS ALAMOS

IN THE SHADOW OF LOS ALAMOS

Selected Writings of Edith Warner

EDITED BY PATRICK BURNS

University of New Mexico Press
Albuquerque

Library of Congress Cataloging-in-Publication Data

Warner, Edith, 1893-1951.
    In the shadow of Los Alamos : selected writings of Edith Warner /
edited by Patrick Burns.—1st ed.
      p.   cm.
Includes bibliographical references.
    ISBN 0-8263-1974-2
    1. Warner, Edith, 1893-1951.   2. Los Alamos Region (N.M.)—
Biography.   3. Los Alamos Region (N.M.)—Description and travel.
4. Los Alamos Region (N.M.)—Social life and customs—20th century.
5. Tearooms—New Mexico—Los Alamos Region—History—20th
century.   6. Restaurateurs—New Mexico—Los Alamos Region—
Biography.   7. Women authors—New Mexico—Los Alamos
Region—Biography.   8. Warner family.   9. Pueblo Indians—New
Mexico—Los Alamos Region—History—20th century.   I. Burns,
Patrick, 1952–   II. Title.
    F804.L6 .W37 2001
    978.9′5805—dc21

                                 2001002383

CONTENTS

Edith Warner

ACKNOWLEDGMENTS

To Stephanie, for the encouragement and support, and four women from whom I gathered much of this story: Lois Bradbury, elementary music teacher, wife of second Los Alamos National Laboratory director Norris Bradbury; Peggy Pond Church, poet, biographer of Edith Warner and Mary Austin, daughter of Ashley Pond, a founder of the Los Alamos Ranch School and wife of Fermor Church, headmaster and teacher at the school; Henrietta ("Peter") Myers Miller, Edith's goddaughter and artist; and Velma Warner Ludlow, Edith's younger sister.

I would also like to thank: Jan Funk, for her work in saving Edith Warner's letters to Peter, and Dr. Robert Myers, Peter's nephew, for permission to use them; Kathleen Church, daughter-in-law and literary executor of Peggy Pond Church, for giving permission to use Peggy Pond Church's papers at UNM and help with proofreading; Joan Chernock for word processing barely legible documents; Los

Alamos Historical Society director Hedy Dunn and former archivist Theresa Strottman, for their help with research and proofreading; Dr. Harold Agnew, third Los Alamos National Laboratory director, who wrote a short memoir of Edith and Tilano; Elizabeth Hadas, Barbara Guth, Amy Elder, Dawn Hall, Melissa Tandysh, and the rest of the staff at UNM Press who gave encouragement and helped shape this book; Karen Taschek, for the great copyediting job; and so many others who helped in so many ways—heartfelt thanks to all.

What we do anywhere matters, but especially here. It matters
very much. Mesas and mountains, rivers and trees, winds and
rains are as sensitive to the actions and thoughts of humans
as we are to their forces. They take into themselves what we
give off, and give it out again.

—*Edith Warner*

$\mathcal{W}$hile reading Peggy Pond Church's biography of Edith Warner, *The House at Otowi Bridge,* I discovered Edith's own writing, and the quest that led to this book began. The eight Christmas letters in the appendix of Church's book, penned by Edith, were my favorite part. To savor the text, I made copies and carried them around with me for months.

Ms. Church wrote in the foreword of her book: "Besides the unfinished manuscript and the handful of Christmas letters, a few typed pages of her journal are all Edith felt willing to leave behind in writing."[1] I wanted to find this original work. I'd read the Frank Waters novel, *The Woman at Otowi Crossing,* years before reading *The House at Otowi Bridge.* In addition to these two books, many pages of writing in newspapers, magazines, and books have explored the life of this fascinating woman. Many people in various genres have told Edith's story. "She is mentioned in sometimes reverent, sometimes romantic, sometimes awestruck terms in nearly every account," wrote journalist Anne Poore.[2] People reinvent and pass along this story as they see fit.

This book contains Edith Warner's own words. Few people realize Edith was a serious lifelong writer herself. This is how she saw her place in the world—her "real" work. The first mention of Edith Warner in *The WPA Guide to 1930s New Mexico* is as a writer.[3] A couple of pages later the guidebook listing continues: " 'EDITH WARNER'S TEAROOM' (overnight accommodations for a limited number arranged in advance), the only place along this part of the route where lunches, teas, and dinners are served."[4] This description is how everyone else saw her: the quiet hostess with a tearoom and picturesque guest house, serving fresh homegrown food and fabulous chocolate cake. Edith described herself as in the business of "feeding folks—though not perhaps in the usual way."[5] Her toil, in what she called her "war-work,"[6] often kept her from the typewriter.

Edith's decision to live in New Mexico was driven by a love of the awe-inspiring scenery, by the gentle power of the ancient and living indigenous cultures, and—most important—by her desire for a simple, quiet life away from the bustle of the East. She knew she couldn't go back. Otowi was where she wanted to be, and she worked hard to survive in this isolated spot, with no indoor water or electricity and only wood for heat and cooking.

When the top-secret Manhattan Project came to the "Hill" in Los Alamos, her quiet was suddenly shattered. Fate brought the birth of the atomic bomb and the beginnings of the Cold War to the mesa above Edith Warner's tearoom. J. Robert Oppenheimer, the director of the Manhattan Project, had often visited the Pajarito Plateau in earlier years, and his friendship with Edith Warner began long before he moved to Los Alamos. Later, her little restaurant became a refuge for the elite cast of young geniuses that Oppenheimer had assembled with the gruesome goal of developing a device with destructive power never before imagined. Edith was not only living at the bridge, she was the bridge between the ancient communal lifestyle of the San Ildefonso Pueblo and the new community of scientists and engineers soon to bring about a new era in the history of mankind. Twin volcanic explosions formed the Pajarito Plateau, and this wonderful high-desert country attracted Edith Warner to New Mexico. The twin man-made atomic explosions that destroyed Hiroshima and Nagasaki were created in nearly the same place. Destiny allowed her to look through keyholes into the past and future, from the great pueblo age to the atomic age.

Edith Warner was a witness to these dramatic and world-changing events. With the successful creation of the atomic bomb, her world and ours changed forever. Unfortunately, we all now live in the shadow of Los Alamos—"the Atomic City."

But even after reading everything I could find about Edith Warner, I still had no clear idea what this woman was really like. I wanted to know more. What did she write? Where were the journals, letters, and unfinished manuscripts stored? I hunted through historical archives in Los Alamos, Santa Fe, and Albuquerque. I was told that in writer Mary Austin's papers there was a copy of Edith's unfinished autobiography, so I tried to track that down. I found out it was "lost" in storage. While digging through Peggy Pond Church's papers for Edith's work, I found a librarian's note next to the listing of Edith Warner's writings—"missing 9/23/94." I searched through libraries, archives, and personal collections. I interviewed, plowed, and scrounged for any small tidbit of the missing writing. I got copies of copies. Each letter or photo, often with handwritten notes on the back, added more pieces to the puzzle and fueled the fire that made me want to search for more. It felt like a treasure hunt.

I began to realize the significance of the untold story I was discovering. There was more writing than I expected to find. Edith had at least eight articles printed in publications that no longer exist. There were pieces of prose dating from when she first came to New Mexico as a visitor in 1922. She continued writing, revising, and editing throughout her life. Edith selected and typed some personal journal entries dated from 1928 through 1935, a few of which were featured in a literary magazine called *Space*. Typed and handwritten letters, in her careful cursive that she called her scrawl, slowly came to light. Encouraged by friends, Edith had begun her autobiography, called *In the Shadow of Los Alamos*. She applied for a grant to complete it, but the project was abandoned. I found other articles she had written, mostly about pueblo life, that she was sending around to editors, hoping for publication.

I wanted to see Edith's writing published with appropriate photographs to enhance the text. Thus began another wonderful search through private collections and great archives of historical photos. I found what I was looking for, including many photos from Edith's personal collection. I couldn't believe that for all these years, the two well-known portrayals in the southwestern classics by Peggy Pond Church and Frank Waters were still selling briskly while Edith's own words had sat on dusty shelves and in boxes. This book is the legacy of Edith Warner, and it is time for her to have her work in print. These words are her petroglyphs. At last, here are the writings of Edith Warner.

INTRODUCTION

The Mystery

$\mathscr{T}$he legend of Edith Warner, who lived by the Rio Grande at the Otowi Switch, began while she was alive and has continued to grow over the years. In the nearly half century since her death, tales about this enigmatic woman and her tearoom by the old suspension bridge have created an aura of mystery about her.

Much of the mystery stems from what has been published about Edith. Frank Waters and Peggy Pond Church, both beloved southwestern writers and characters in their own right, produced two very different portraits of Edith with similar titles—Waters's *The Woman at Otowi Crossing* and Church's *The House at Otowi Bridge*. Both books reveal some aspects of Edith Warner's life, but neither really tells her own story.

The Waters novel focuses on the spiritual development of the heroine, Helen Chalmers (Edith). Spirituality was certainly a major aspect of Edith's life. Many people feel that through a series of mystic experiences, Edith Warner had reached a union with a deeper self—a form of enlightenment—and just being near her could affect a person spiritually. Edith wrote in her journal on March 2, 1933, "Just now it seemed to flow in a rhythm around me and then to enter me—that something which comes in a hushed inflowing. All of me is still and yet alert, ready to become a part of this wave that laps the shore on which I sit. Somehow I have no desire to name it or understand. It is enough that I should feel and be of it in moments such as this." Edith was a Baptist minister's daughter who loved to read and had access to and an understanding of the ancient religion of her neighbors at the San Ildefonso Pueblo, a combination that created her unique brand of spirituality. "We knew others were touched and helped," Edith's sister Velma told Peggy Church, "but was it as strongly spiritual to them as to us?"[1] Edith's goddaughter, Henrietta ("Peter") Myers Miller, wrote that her husband, Earle, "was so much in awe of [Edith] (I think most men felt that way about her)." Peter accepted Edith as her spiritual mentor. "I believe most eastern religions say when you are ready a teacher will come," Peter wrote. "I believe [Edith] was as close to becoming as completely free of self as anyone I've known."[2] Another friend said, "[Edith] was a sort of religion herself."[3]

Edith believed that true knowledge was for all—as a group, not as single individuals. Much of her fascination with the religion of Native Americans had to do with group beliefs and consciousness. She may have been intrigued by the esprit de corps that her new neighbors in Los Alamos shared, although she didn't know what they were doing.

Although she was a deeply spiritual person, Edith would never have considered herself a prophet. She loved the phrase "flute of the gods" and wrote, "I had no particular power but acted as [a] medium through which [a] source of strength could flow." In a letter to her goddaughter she said, "If a man brought about a renaissance it did not outlive him because it was he and not the people. Christ tried to make his teachings the important thing but people used the crucifixion to make it him. . . . Perhaps the time approaches when the people must act as groups. . . . Nothing comes by leaps and bounds but by years. Eventually one should be able to make a high place within, but not for one's own use. . . . The knowledge that I thought was beyond man's compass can be so strong in a human being that it radiates and yet it does not make him a 'master.'"[4]

Waters began *The Woman at Otowi Crossing* and worked on it for fifteen years before Swallow Press published it in 1966. It was revised, trimmed, and rejected by several publishers. In his papers there are six versions spread out in boxes and chapters buried in files of correspondence. Waters deleted hundreds of pages, working the text like a piece of sculpture. He explained: "For one reason they were afraid to do it after the Oppenheimer controversy; they were afraid a lot of that was classified material and then they objected to the religious theme that ran through it."[5]

Frank Waters was reluctantly willing to compromise to get his novel published. He said, "Finally in desperation . . . I cut it down—but I cut it down too much. I've been sorry about that ever since. And I think the time will come when I can put back . . . some of the stuff I took out."[6] A revised edition was printed in 1987 with some of the deleted text. The revised edition was reprinted in 1998 with a new introduction by Professor Emeritus Thomas J. Lyon and a foreword by Waters's widow, Barbara.

Lawrence Clark Powell remarked in the magazine *Westways:* "In 1966 [Frank] Waters outraged New Mexican opinion with a novel, *The Woman at Otowi Crossing.* . . . The uproar came from his book's having followed Peggy Pond Church's *The House at Otowi Bridge,* a poetic biography of Miss Warner and her Indian friend, Tilano. Their relationship was said to have been platonic. Waters did not believe that it was, and he proceeded in his book to give Edith Warner an Anglo lover [named Jack Turner] somewhat modeled on himself."[7]

Other fictions in the Waters book include Helen Chalmers leaving her alcoholic millionaire husband and infant daughter, Emily, behind when she moves to New Mexico. Emily grows up in a "huge, twenty-room grey stoned mansion"[8] and leads a pampered blue blood's life in East Coast society. Attending upper-crust private schools, Emily studies anthropology. This interest leads her to New Mexico and her mother. Edith Warner never married, had no children, and worked very hard to make a living. She was proud to be called Miss Warner.

Edith's goddaughter, Peter, who was probably the person that the character Emily was based on, wrote to Frank Waters in 1966, "You must have known Edith Warner very slightly, if at all, to have done her such a disservice. The true story was so beautiful that it needed no embellishments to popularize it. That is the last thing she would have wanted. . . . I wish you hadn't done it."[9] Waters's reply to Peter has not been found, but in interviews he said, "I . . . knew Edith Warner. We used to go down there, several of us from Taos, and picnic up the canyon and always stop by the tearoom to have her berry pie or chocolate cake. I always thought she was a very lovely woman and a very fey woman. And living as she did just presented right away a novel."[10] "I changed her name and her life. This is not a biography. But it is the story of the myth about her that has grown up and is believed by her Spanish and Indian neighbors."[11] Peter replied to Waters, "You answered very kindly saying that the liberties you took with her life and character were adopted in order to immortalize her. It seems to me a dubious blessing to be immortalized inaccurately. I have heard from several sources that the fantasies in your book are now being repeated as facts of her life. You are wrong in saying she would mind this less than her friends. She would mind terribly."[12]

Scholar Charles L. Adams recalls on a trip to Taos with a friend to meet Frank Waters the friend saying to Waters: "'I've just finished reading a biography of Edith Warner by Peggy Pond Church. . . . I've been wondering which one is the true one.' Waters thought for a moment, then answered, 'Peggy Church's book is a biography; my book is a novel. Her book is fact; mine is fiction. Hers deals with history; mine is imaginative.' Then after a pause, and a grin I'll always remember, he looked at us and said, 'Mine is the true one.'"[13] Waters felt that Church was a "very fine poet" but pointed out, "*The House at Otowi Bridge* is . . . autobiography, principally."[14]

Peggy Pond Church's book also provides an incomplete and somewhat biased picture of Edith's life. Church's endeavor to "join the broken threads of [Edith's] story together and weave them with my own"[15] was in reality an opportunity to confront her own feelings and tell her own story. Author Shelley Armitage wrote that Church "found in 'the woman who dwells in singing by the river' (Warner's Indian name) an antidote to her own turbulent, sometimes bitter, and rebellious self. They knew each other during the years when the development of nuclear warfare not only threatened human life worldwide but forced Church and her husband to leave the Los Alamos Ranch School where he taught—disinherited from their land on the Pajarito Plateau where the beauty of New Mexico and the visible history of the Anasazi had been Church's heritage since girlhood. In her moving depiction of Warner, Church reveals her own coming into self-understanding, 'the worth of my own woman's life.' In her book, published in 1959, eight years after Warner's death from cancer, the biographer examines her own life in light of her subject's life and writings and of their friendship."[16]

Like almost everyone else, Peggy Church seemed in awe of Edith Warner. Church admitted in her journal that Edith was "the only woman I know with whom I would exchange lives. She has the kind of life I would like to have."[17] Church wrote, "The trouble with the book—I could not be truly objective. I kept connecting Edith with me."[18] "I have muddied your image."[19]

Peggy Church began work on her book in 1955. She received a Longview Literary Award for her portrait of Edith that was first published in the *New Mexico Quarterly*. She expanded the text and sent rough drafts to friends and family for approval as she researched and wrote her most well known work. In response, Edith's sister Velma wrote to Church, "You create such a wonderfully clear picture of Edith and Tilano in the first few pages. . . . The story of your father, the school, and your early married life [is] another story entirely."[20] Velma suggested, "If you could give the picture of Otowi as it was when she first went there and build it up to the time of the [Christmas] letters, then put in the letters and conclude with a final chapter, do you think that would do justice to the story? Would it upset you to do it this way . . . ? It would mean a completely new approach."[21]

The University of New Mexico Press at first rejected Church's text. She kept at it, rewriting her book with many different working titles, including *Finished in Beauty, Neighbor to Los Alamos,* and *By the Road to Los Alamos.* After "valiant use of . . . editorial scissors,"[22] Church wrote in her chronology, "THE BRIDGE IS OUT!"[23] In its thirteenth printing in 1998, the book is a southwestern classic.

Peggy Pond Church wrote to Frank Waters in 1966: "The first time I read *The Woman at Otowi Crossing* it made me sort of sick; the second time it made me a little mad; the third time I read it slowly and carefully during a day in bed and found much in it. . . . I regret the hurt . . . but time will doubtless heal that. . . . One of these days you and I will run into one another in our comings and goings around Santa Fe and I hope for the sake of many things we have in common that we can meet as friends and leave controversy to the level where it belongs."[24] Charles Adams tells of a party in Taos where the host purposely invited both writers without letting them know the other would be there to see what would happen. Waters and Church were both very cordial and friendly.[25]

The controversy between the fans of Frank Waters and Peggy Church continues.[26] Both sides claim the writers stole titles and ideas from each other and were in a race to get their manuscripts published first. The competition supposedly began when Waters asked Church for copies of Edith's Christmas letters for the novel he was working on. There's no evidence that she gave them to him, but he got them somewhere—I found some copies in his files. Many in the Church camp refuse to read the Waters book, whereas some scholars hail the Waters book as an American masterpiece comparable to *Moby Dick.*

Like all legends, the story of Edith Warner's life changes with the storyteller. "No one could really tell the whole story [of Edith Warner]. . . . One interpretation of her would not fit another's remembrance of her," Edith's old friend Winifred Fisher said.[27] Velma Warner similarly cautioned: "Interpretation . . . may spoil [Edith's story] for someone else."[28]

This book presents Edith Warner's own words. This is her opportunity to set the record somewhat straight about who she was and what she felt and saw. But in a way, this book will also add to the controversy. Edith Warner was a complex and clairvoyant woman who realized the irony and interest of her life story. She knew early on that she was on a spiritual journey and eagerly sought another level of understanding beyond that of most women or men of her generation. She followed destiny to the Rio Grande, and in this solitude she nurtured an inner growth. She adopted a way of living and thinking that was at odds with everyday life in her culture, as was her pursuit of a kind of knowing that doesn't measure and probe. That she was so quiet just added to the myth. Perhaps unconsciously Edith helped to create the image of herself that made her so enchanting to others.

PART I

Historical Overview

THE WARNER FAMILY

They had helped me as long as they could, and then had
become resigned to my solving the problem alone. They must
have had faith in the Lord—and perhaps some in me, for they
had never put any obstacles in my way.

—*Edith Warner, unfinished autobiography*

Reverend Charles Pierre Warner, born on September 27, 1864, in
Philadelphia,[1] "was shy but independent as could be," his daughter
Velma said.[2] His ancestry was English, Welsh, and Scotch.[3] "A small,
gentle, man . . . He must always have given the effect of fragility and
timidity. He had not started out to be a preacher, and was, in fact,
fairly well in some business when he suddenly decided that the ministry was for him. He was married and two of his children had been
born, so it was a momentous decision. In some way he managed to
get through divinity school and a change. . . . Preaching was always

a torture for him, but he drove himself to it," Edith's goddaughter, Peter, recalled.[4] "Edith was 10 years old by the time my father became a minister," Velma said, describing his drive as "father's determination."[5] His granddaughter, Sue Smith, remembered him as potbellied and very strict. He continued his Baptist ministry in Pottstown and retired in Bryn Mawr.[6]

Charles's wife, Ida F. Mayer, was born in Reading on November 19, 1866.[7] Of German stock, Ida "was a dynamic woman of physical strength and great will. She had great ability to work with people, organization, understanding, and [was] almost psychic. She always knew things without our telling her," Velma said. She remembered her "mother's tremendous pride . . . charm and understanding, gentleness and humility. . . . A tower of strength to my father (his greatest admirer and severest critic)."[8]

The Warners' first child and only son, Paul Mayer, was born on November 6, 1891, and died very young.[9] Edith Mayer Warner joined the family on August 22, 1893, in Philadelphia.[10] "None of the rest of us is as good a combination of our parents as Edith was," Velma said. "She was an only child for seven years—spent almost entirely with adults, and especially with my grandfather, and she was a very serious child, reading books quite early and seldom playing with dolls or toys. . . . Of Edith's childhood I really know very little, she being 10 years older than I."[11] All Edith's goddaughter could add about those early years was: "Everything she ever said about that period of her life sounded completely unhappy."[12]

Four more girls were born to the Warners: Florence Haley, in Philadelphia, on December 3, 1899; Elizabeth ("Dib") Laurens, in Philadelphia, on June 8, 1901; Velma Mowen, in Loch Haven, on December 8, 1902; and Mary Horz, in Pottstown, on December 12, 1909.[13] The responsibilities of family life as the oldest sister certainly kept Edith busy. This was especially true on Sundays, when Charles had his duties at church. He was known to "volunteer" the girls for tasks like washing dishes for the ladies at the church. None of the daughters were supposed to go to movies on Sundays, but sometimes they went anyway, telling their father they were off to the theater. He would laugh because he thought they were pulling his leg.[14]

After high school, Edith graduated from Lock Haven State Normal School in 1910.[15] She taught both elementary- and secondary-level children. "The teaching experience was worst of all—she despised it—everything about it, and used to tell me how each morning she'd stand miserably on a street corner, waiting for a bus to come along and take her to school, wondering how she could manage to live through another day of it," Edith's goddaughter wrote.[16]

Edith found a new job as a secretary at the YWCA "as the result of the influence of two women in Pottstown who were on the board of the YWCA with Mother and who sensed her ability to be of help to others,"[17] Velma wrote. Peter said, "It was not quite so bad [as teaching]. At least that involved a lot of outdoor life—they went camping and picnicking—and she was fond of some of the girls—but even so it was wrong for her and she knew it. Fortunately her body revolted, I'm sure she never could have escaped in any other way. She always had a certain feeling of guilt about not having done 'her share' of helping her parents."[18] Edith suffered a nervous breakdown in 1921. Perhaps the responsibilities expected from being the oldest sister, combined with problems finding a suitable career, were the reasons. "I go up and down," she wrote at the end of a letter to a friend, possibly an indication of mood swings.[19] Whatever the causes, "her young womanhood wasn't gay—she was conscious of the lack," Peter wrote. "Her doctors said that she must go somewhere where she could live quietly and be out of doors."[20] Edith came to New Mexico when she was twenty-nine. She said and wrote very little about her first twenty-nine years in Pennsylvania. "Edith's earlier years are not important," Velma said. "It is what happened while she was actually in New Mexico that matters."[21]

NEW MEXICO-ITIS

I wonder if these cliffs that have been reflecting the old sun's rays all through the years know how they calm the ruffled, troubled soul of me? I wonder if the people who lived in these cliff caves so long ago felt as I do the sureness, the timelessness of them and so walked calmly through life. When I come here and sit on the stone worn smooth and a bit hollowed by moccasined feet, with my back against one cliff, so solid and assuring, around me the entrances to caves where people lived, loved and died, my mind clears as do troubled waters when the sand ... s to the bottom of the pool.

—*Edith Warner, "Fiesta Time at San Ildefonso"*

*W*hen Edith first came to New Mexico for rest and recuperation in October 1922, "she seems to have chosen New Mexico almost at random. A friend of hers had been there," her goddaughter wrote.[1]

Miss Warner came to live with trader John Boyd and his wife, Martha, at their ranch in Frijoles Canyon for almost a year.

Much of this country is southwest of the Valle Grande, the world's largest extinct volcanic crater, measuring 176 square miles in the Jemez Mountains. The volcano that formed the Valle Caldera blew about a million years ago, spewing lava that became fingerlike tuff formations at the base of the mountains, called the Jemez Plateau. One of these tuff formations, narrow Frijoles ("beans") Canyon, has a rare year-round creek that makes an oasis lush with wildlife at the canyon bottom. A six-hundred-foot vertical climb out of the canyon leads to piñon, juniper, ponderosa pine, and aspen forests with more than five hundred recorded plant species. Wildlife, from the rare Jemez Mountain salamander to mountain lions, is also abundant.

The Boyds' land, once part of the Ramón Vigil Land Grant, is now part of Bandelier National Monument, named after Adolph Bandelier, the renowned Swiss scientist-novelist who explored the remains of the ancient Americans who thrived there. Visiting in 1880, he wrote, "It is the grandest thing I ever saw."[2] Bandelier spent only two weeks there, but through their writings, he and Dr. Edgar L. Hewett made the nation aware of this magnificent archaeological resource in New Mexico. Of the approximately seven thousand archaeological sites identified in the monument, only a few hundred have been officially excavated. Remains of huge adobe pueblos adorn the mesa tops and cliff sides as the spirits of the Anasazi waft past in the air. The south-facing cliff houses carved in soft pumice are surrounded by pit houses below. In the canyons of Pajarito Plateau are the ruins of an amazing network of ancient cities connected by extensive roads: in Frijoles Canyon almost seventeen miles of cliff dwellings are sculpted in the soft rock.

This majestic country has drawn people since about 9500 B.C., when the isolation, natural protection, and beauty of the Pajarito Plateau attracted the first Keres-speaking people. They lived in caves and moved on to settle in Cochiti, Santo Domingo, San Felipe, Santa Ana, Acoma, Laguna, and Zia. About a century later the first Tewa-speaking peoples, who were the ancestors of the San Ildefonsans, came from Chaco Canyon and Mesa Verde. The population on the Pajarito Plateau grew to about five thousand. In the 1300s some of these people began moving closer to the Rio Grande, and by about A.D. 1515 all that remained on the Pajarito Plateau were extensive ruins, including abandoned pueblos at Navawi, Tshirege, Tsankawi, Otowi, Totavi, and Puye.

Peggy Pond Church dubbed the love of this area "New Mexico-itis."[3] Not surprisingly, Edith embraced the place. From her first visit, Edith displayed a keen awareness for this country that she would later call home. She was fascinated with the landscape and culture of the Native Americans who have thrived here for ages.

Edith's money ran out after a year with the Boyds, but she hoped to stay in New Mexico. She'd fallen in love with a cowboy named Pete, who planned to become a forest ranger. They both enjoyed hiking in the forests of the Jemez Mountains and the rowdy Hispanic dances in nearby Jemez Springs. They took pack trips together with Edith's friend Ann Sherman and the Boyds' son Jim.[4] Edith convinced her sister Velma to come to Albuquerque in the fall of 1923. A rendezvous was planned with Pete in the Pecos for a camping trip in August 1924. "He came—but to tell her it was all off! I was too young to really appreciate the tragedy of it, and in love myself, so blind I guess," Velma wrote. "Edith had a number of serious love affairs in her younger years which didn't materialize. . . . There were several men . . . who wanted to marry her, but it wasn't part of the picture. She knew love and heartbreak. As I look back, they were all steps she climbed to become the person she was."[5] Velma and Edith stayed in Albuquerque at the YWCA until the summer of 1924. Velma was also enchanted with New Mexico but returned east to wed Benjamin Ludlow. She eventually moved back and spent her later years in Santa Fe. All the Warner sisters, except Florence, who had died, spent some time living in New Mexico.[6]

In late August of 1924 Edith went to stay with the Smithwicks, friends she had met during her stay in Frijoles Canyon, to recover from her breakup with Pete. Frank and Constance (Connie) Smithwick lived at Anchor Ranch, a few miles south of Los Alamos.

Edith extended her stay, helping tutor and look after a boy with special needs named Alex who lived with the Smithwicks. Edith once remarked to Connie, "I can't even boil water!"[7] but Connie realized that Edith simply hadn't learned the art of starting and maintaining a fire in a wood cookstove. Connie wrote in a letter to Peggy Church, "Our never-fail chocolate cake was our one success."[8] After her stay at Anchor Ranch, Edith returned east. She traveled to Florida as a companion to an elderly woman and spent the winter there.

Edith became a patient at the Tilden Health School in Denver, which advocated dietary practices and fasting for good health. She remained as a part of the staff for several years, and in the summer of 1925, her writing was first published in the center's journal, *The Philosophy of Health*. Edith's time at Tilden changed her both physically and spiritually. She lost weight and became very aware of what and how she ate. She learned meditation, how to relax and breathe properly. In the 1920s, she was already "New Age."

Unable to stay away from New Mexico, Edith was back in Santa Fe in 1928, looking for some kind of work. She wanted to live in north-central New Mexico but had no luck in her job search. Tired of hauling around crates of books and her typewriter, she almost gave up and returned east.[9]

LOS ALAMOS RANCH SCHOOL

Mr. Connell, director of the school, was an Irishman who usually obtained his objective, whether that was a boy for the
school or a lawn in a dry land. He went to Santa Fe determined
to find a responsible man who would stay at Otowi Station,
but unfortunately no one wanted to live way out there with
the only inducement an assured income of twenty-five dollars
monthly. During the evening he chanced to see me at La
Fonda, in Santa Fe. I also was determined—determined to find
some way of earning a living in New Mexico.

—Edith Warner, unfinished autobiography

$\mathcal{M}$r. A. J. Connell negotiated the treacherous turns down that dan-
gerous and rapidly growing worse road[1] and found what little was
left of the supplies and mail for his school left by the Denver and Rio
Grande Western Railroad strewn in front of the abandoned boxcar

at Otowi. He went on to San Ildefonso and parked his truck under a large cottonwood tree by the old plaza. When he was greeted with wide smiles and his Tewa name, Bo-Ah-Gi Cha I, it cheered him up some. He was proud to have his own name at the pueblo, although he didn't know that it meant "Baby Pants" because he always wore shorts.[2] He was looking for someone to replace Adam, son of San Ildefonso's famous potters Maria and Julian, who used to watch the deliveries. Connell gave up and headed to Santa Fe to find someone reliable to do the job. That's where he ran into Edith.

Connell's school had a reputation as a unique place to toughen up boys through a rigorous regimen. Except for two short rest periods after meals, the daily schedule for the boys at the school was planned from 6:30 A.M. exercises to 7:00 P.M. lights-out with "practically no outside diversions."[3] With a tough curriculum that included Latin and physics, Connell's main goal was to improve the health of the boys. Shorts were the year-round uniforms, and all the boys slept out-of-doors in sleeping porches—even during bitter winter cold. Each boy was assigned a horse and saddle. Connell had realized his dream while employed by the Forest Service of a mounted school modeled on the principles of the Boy Scouts of America. The facility had a six-year program gearing graduates for the best colleges, such as Cornell, Harvard, Princeton, and Yale. The Ranch School had grown from three students in 1918 to forty-seven boys ages twelve to eighteen. The spectacular setting on 750 acres on the Pajarito Plateau mesa was originally part of the Ramón Vigil Grant.

Fermor Church, former headmaster, wrote in the *Harvard College Class of 1921 Twenty-fifth Anniversary Report*: "The unique features of Los Alamos School were those which were indigenous—its program and its spirit stemmed from its surroundings. No circumscribed, artificial campus life could develop here before the beckoning attractions of forest, stream, canyon, mesa, and mountain-peak—with horse at hand. And amid the ruined cities of early pueblo and cliff-dweller we felt and knew that the thing men live for never dies."[4]

Fuller Lodge, named after benefactor Edward Fuller, was added in 1928. The beautiful three-story ponderosa pine log structure designed by architect John Gaw Meem was the center of campus life. The Ashley Pond, named after one of the founders, was used for sports and recreational activities.

Fermor Church, at that time the school's math and science teacher, married Peggy Pond, Ashley's daughter, who was living in Santa Fe. Peggy knew the area well, and the couple had three sons. Other than the nurse and Peggy Church, there were no women at the school. Connell often made Peggy feel uncomfortable because he didn't want any female influence on the boys. Sometimes she would escape to Otowi to visit Edith and Tilano.

The war was first felt at the school after the invasion of Pearl Harbor. First headmaster Fayette Curtis was drafted for active duty, and Fermor took his place. Soon other teachers were called into the service. One fateful day, General Leslie R. Groves, head of the Army Corps of Engineers, visited the school with Dr. J. Robert Oppenheimer (who was never a student, as many people believe) to inspect it as a possible site for a top-secret project. Groves liked what he saw. They had also considered Oak City, Utah, and Jemez Springs, New Mexico, but chose the mesa where Los Alamos Ranch School was situated because of its isolation and beauty. Fermor Church wrote, "We rebuffed all advances made by army real-estate men, engineers, scientists, and inspectors of all sorts until a letter from the Secretary of War [Henry Stimson] left us no choice. We were told on December 7, 1942, that our entire property was necessary to the government and the United States would exercise the right of eminent domain to secure it."[5] The school hastily arranged a midyear graduation for the last four seniors. Fermor tried to relocate the school to the present-day Sagebrush Inn in Taos but was unsuccessful in his efforts to keep the school going. All that's left of Los Alamos Ranch School today is the newly restored Fuller Lodge, the Los Alamos Historical Museum, and the privately owned faculty housing that's still called "bathtub row," due to the lack of bathtubs in early wartime Los Alamos housing. Downstairs at "The Lodge" are an art center and the Pajarito Room, where the boys would warm up by the big fireplace and study. The second floor is home to the

Los Alamos Historical Society, which is full of photographs and memories of the once thriving, unique school. A bit of the influence of Boy Scout leader Connell remains today on some boys in Los Alamos through Troop 22.

Station agent!

THE CHILI LINE

I went back to the funny car with its oil lamps, heatless stove
and narrow seats, where, wrapped in coat and sweater . . . we
were off into the southland. The engine seemed to crawl, but
glimpses of far-away mountains and wondering about my
neighbors made me forget, at intervals, the long journey
ahead, the stale air, my cold feet. At one little station and
another, we had been added to until there was quite a cross
section of humanity in that now crowded coach.

—*Edith Warner, "Narrow Gauge Meals,"*
Philosophy of Health, *May 1926*

The Denver and Rio Grande Western Railroad (D&RGW) would
hardly reach the average speed of about seventeen miles per hour
before grinding to another stop on the 125-mile trip from Antonito,
Colorado, to Santa Fe that ran round-trip every day but Sunday. Begun

in the 1880s, the plan was for the little train to eventually link Denver to Mexico City. It was the first railway in America to use three-foot, or "narrow-gauge," track. New Mexico historian Marc Simmons wrote: "Among the most spectacular and historic of the old feeder lines . . . the train gave riders extraordinary scenic views and a hair-raising thrill as it descended the steep grade into the Rio Grande Canyon. It was popularly known as the 'Chili Line,' because it passed through some of New Mexico's finest chili-growing country."[1] Georgia Maryol, restaurateur at Tomasita's Santa Fe Station—the final destination of the Chili Line—wrote, "Its seventeen hour run . . . through mountain, mesa and river valley connected villages, pueblos, towns and cultures. The D&RG was the timekeeper, the newspaper, the friend of children and the transporter of local goods—lumber, piñon, wool, chili and fruit. Due to the decline in the demand for lumber, traffic on the line was greatly reduced in the 30s."[2]

A suspension bridge across the Rio Grande had been built at Otowi in 1921 by the Union Bridge Company, and a boxcar was left to store the supplies that were dropped off three times a week for the Los Alamos Ranch School. The bridge replaced the old Buckman Bridge to the south, which began collapsing in 1917, the same year the school began. Otowi became a post office in 1923. Macario "Shorty" Pelaez was the first stationmaster.[3] Shorty opened a small store featuring bootleg booze. From 1928 to 1941, Edith Warner was the station agent who met the train at Otowi. She wrote in her unfinished autobiography: "My ideas of how I might earn a living in a sparsely inhabited country had been numerous but not practical for an unmarried woman of thirty-five with no capital. Certainly those ideas had not included taking care of freight or selling gasoline and Coca-Cola in an ugly frame house at Otowi Bridge." Velma said Edith had envisioned a "house by the side of the road where she could provide rest, peace and a proper diet. I'm sure she didn't know how it was possible or perhaps it was a subconscious seed but surely it was what she succeeded in doing for many plus a spiritual renewal."[4] Edith worked hard fixing up the decrepit house. She sold refreshments, like her chocolate cake and soft drinks. The meager $25 monthly sum the school paid her took care of the rent with a little left to pay Adam to unload the cargo. She also read the river gauge for the state. Edith opened a tearoom where she served meals, and the extra bedroom was rented to guests. In the late 1920s the train was scheduled to leave Otowi at 1:00 P.M. on the journey to Santa Fe, but as John A. Gjevre noted in his book *The Chili Line,* "Often the crews would stop for a leisurely snack or soft drink. (Timetables were perhaps meant to be stretched a bit)."[5] Although Edith Warner wasn't an employee of the D&RGW, Otowi became a famous stop on the Chili Line thanks to the station mistress. Tourism was up as more people visited Bandelier, and Edith began expanding her business as "the tempo of daily life increased. . . . Building [a] guest house—[was] a long slow process by Indians."[6] The guest house, which was also known as Tilano's house, was finished in 1934.

With the advent of the war in Europe and the high labor costs of steam trains, business suddenly dried up. Bankruptcy was inevitable. The train had been operating in the red, and passengers dwindled to about ten a trip. "Miss Warner's tearoom business had folded in part due to the war but more specifically because of the demise of the railroad, which had previously stopped nearby to pick up water for its steam engine. Ironically the removal and transfer of the railroad to Alaska had been under the direction of General Groves who built Los Alamos," third Los Alamos Laboratory director Harold Agnew wrote.[7] The Army Corps of Engineers tore up the tracks and shipped them where the old Chili Line could move supplies for our allies in Russia. The remaining narrow gauge lines, Chama–Antonito and Durango–Silverton, now cater to tourists and are two of the most popular tourist trains in North America, but the struggle to remain in the black continues. The Chili Line probably would have survived if Groves had any idea what fate had in store for him and Los Alamos.

PO-WOH-GE-OWEENGE
(PUEBLO DE SAN ILDEFONSO)

I keep thinking of those prehistoric people who left the
Plateau during a long drought, left the pueblos where we find
potsherds and arrow points in the rubble. They, too, must have
scanned the sky with hope and finally with despair before
they decided to leave their homes and sacred places, to journey to the south. As the Pueblo tale of their ancestors goes,
the lazy ones stayed beside the river and made a new home
here in the valley. Were they really lazy or did they have faith
that their ceremonies still had power to bring the rains again?
—*Edith Warner, Christmas Report, 1950*

The Keresans, in about 9500 B.C. the first people to occupy the
natural caves on the Pajarito Plateau, grew corn, beans, and squash
and lived in villages. When the Keresans moved on, about a hundred
years later, the second wave, of Tewa-speaking people, arrived. Towns

with elaborate architecture like Chaco show how advanced this culture became between A.D. 900 and 1300. San Ildefonso, or Po-Woh-Ge-Oweenge (Where the Water Cuts Down Through), was first settled in the 1300s by peoples from Mesa Verde and Bandelier. They probably migrated because of lack of water and soil depletion. The ruins of Otowi show large, multilevel structures, similar in construction to the Taos Pueblo, with ten kivas. The village was first situated on the west bank of the Rio Grande but is now to the east, under large cottonwoods with Pojoaque River to the south. With its vistas of the grand Jemez Mountains to the west, Truchas to the east, and the sacred basaltic Black Mesa (Tunyo) to the north, San Ildefonso occupies a truly spectacular setting.

Agrarian, democratic, and usually peaceful, the village people traded their pots, jewelry, and produce with neighboring tribes. The warriors fought occasional renegade attacks by other tribes, but in general the pueblo didn't focus on warfare. That changed with the coming of the Spanish.[1]

In March 1539 Franciscan friar Marcos de Niza, seeking the wealth of the "Seven Cities of Cíbola," sent a Moroccan slave named Estevan north from Culiacán. The "European" discovery of New Mexico was actually by this large African, who along the way from Mexico had been treated to gifts and women, throwing themselves at what they thought was a god. His party encountered pueblo peoples near Zuni, who discovered that Estevan was not a god and killed him. The following year Vásquez de Coronado led the first Europeans into the Rio Grande Valley, bringing horses and introducing new crops. A party led by Antonio Gutiérrez de Humaña spent much of 1593 at San Ildefonso. In September 1595 Juan de Oñate was awarded a contract to colonize New Mexico at his own expense, and after long travels across the state, he arrived at a village that he named San Ildefonso. That was the beginning of the Spanish settlements in pueblo country.

The newcomers didn't plan to drive out the Native Americans but to Christianize, colonize, and exploit them. Friar Cristóbal de Salazar, a Franciscan, founded a mission and monastery at San

Ildefonso in 1617, and construction with forced labor began on the first beautiful adobe church at the pueblo, financed by heavy taxation. The Spanish considered the Native Americans heathens and sacrilegious and so discouraged traditional religious activity, banned it, or forced it underground. Tensions grew steadily between the Spanish and the Indians in the area until the Pueblo Revolt, led by Popé of San Juan Pueblo, erupted on August 10, 1680. Fray Luis de Morales and his assistant, Antonio Sánchez de Pío, were murdered at the altar at San Ildefonso during services. Padre Morales was said to be well liked by the Indians, but no Spaniard was spared. Diego de Vargas recaptured San Ildefonso in August 1694, and the natives fled to the top of Black Mesa. Although the Indians used only arrows and rocks against the Spaniards' superior firepower, de Vargas finally had to abandon the siege. San Ildefonso seems never to have actually surrendered, although an uneasy peace was declared in 1692. A new mission was established, but on June 4, 1696, Franciscans Fray Francisco Corvera and Fray Antonio Moreño were burned alive in the church and Spanish forces again fought the San Ildefonsans at Black Mesa. This time they were victorious. The pueblo eventually converted to Catholicism, but the San Ildefonso people still treasure their own culture and the traditional religious rites passed on from their ancestors. In 1858 the U.S. government granted 17,292 acres to the Pueblo de San Ildefonso. At the new church, built to replace the one that had burned down, many Catholic celebrations like Christmas and Easter now began with a mass followed by traditional dances.[2]

In 1912, when New Mexico acquired statehood, the pueblos came under the control of the federal government. The U.S. government wanted to bring Native Americans into mainstream American life, and the old ways, including the traditional religious customs, were once again discouraged or banned, and often ceremonies had to be taken underground. The bureaucratic battles for tribal sovereignty continue today as the tribe debates with the state and federal governments over laws regulating road easements, water rights, taxation, and the jurisdiction of tribal courts and police.

During her first visit to New Mexico, Edith Warner wrote in a

photo scrapbook: "January 23, 1923, annual Fiesta at San Ildefonso celebrated by Comanche War Dance. My first experience never to be
forgotten. Dedication of new plaza."[3] This "new" plaza dedication
took place during a very tangled and complex period in the history
of this proud village, when inside stress and encroachments by the
Spanish and the Anglos had created internal turmoil. The problems
had begun many centuries ago, sometime before the Spanish conquest, when the village elders decided to move the village north. Tewa
villages traditionally move to the south, and San Ildefonso had always
followed this custom. But after much prayer and controversy, a decision was made to move the village north toward sacred Tunyo (now
called Black Mesa). This shift changed the positions of the kivas, dis-
rupting the patterns of social and religious order. In 1918, after centuries of dispute and bad feelings, a council of all the Tewa villages
was called. The council decided to move the village back to the south,
within the original boundaries. But many families refused to accept
this decision and remained where they were. According to historian
Marc Simmons, "Bitter factionalism . . . had long plagued San
Ildefonso and caused a deep split. María and Julian Martínez were
involved as were all residents."[4]

The feud didn't keep the pueblo, or Edith, from their religious
practices. The spiritual life and ceremonials at San Ildefonso have
been practiced the same way for generations. The pueblo is traditionally governed by a theocracy, and the cacique, or spiritual leader,
serves for a lifetime. The kiva, or center of the religious ceremonial,
is the center of the village. With its central theme of new or renewed
life, Tewa religion involves all aspects of being, both individual and
social. Religious activities are for the benefit of the entire community. Edith wrote in her journal on October 25, 1933: "This morning at the dawning I stood on the riverbank to pray. I knew then
that the ancient ones were wise to pray for peace and beauty and
not for specific gifts except fertility, which is continued life. And I
saw that if one has even a small degree of the ability to take into and
unto himself the peace and the beauty the gods surround him with,
it is not necessary to ask for more."

Edith Warner's friendships at the village began several years before she rented the lumberman's shack from Maria and Julian. It was like coming home. As her business at Otowi grew, she was able to employ a few villagers to help with her tearoom business and for construction and fix-up work.

The effects of World War II were first felt at the village with the advent of the secret city on the Hill, where the Los Alamos Ranch School was. In 1944 Frijoles Lodge in Bandelier was taken over by the government and run by Dorothy McKibben to house a hundred people working at Los Alamos. As the project at Los Alamos expanded, it brought work to more and more pueblo women, who did domestic duties.

Some of the young men at the pueblo avoided overseas duty through contacts at Los Alamos. Edith wrote in a letter: "S. came over to say goodbye AND so did darling Diego. Only he was refused finally by the army and has taken some kind of course in aviation ground work. He expects to be an INSTRUCTOR!!—and not to be sent out of the country. He would."[5] Maria's son Popovi Da, who was already working in Los Alamos as a civilian, was drafted and stationed in Los Alamos without having to go through basic training. Through ties on the Hill, he was able to continue working in Los Alamos after he was drafted. "The Martinez family plays safe," Edith wrote to her goddaughter. Popovi Da would later serve three times as governor of San Ildefonso. He was also the first Native American to receive a small GI loan, and with this money he established a business with his mother that helped the pueblo realize the monetary value of their art. Artwork is still the financial base of the village.

T I L A N O   A N D   E D I T H

He says little but thinks a lot.

> —*Edith Warner, from a letter to Peter Miller*

*A*tilano ("Tilano") Montoya, Maria Martinez's uncle and former governor and elder at the pueblo, came to build Edith a fireplace in about 1928 and wound up her housemate. He lived out his years at Otowi, and his loving, complex relationship to Edith is an important part of the legend that has grown up around her. He helped with all the work: the garden, animals, woodpile, cooking, serving, and cleanup. "He did the things a man would do," Lois Bradbury said.[1]

According to pueblo lore, Tilano's first stay at Otowi was to dry out from a binge. He became a teetotaler. "She fell in love with Tilano. It wasn't a man and wife situation—the prime interest was spiritual," Peter Miller's childhood friend and former Indian Service employee Heinrich Schultz said.[2] "It was not a romantic situation," agreed writer Kathleen Mark, who was married to one of the original Manhattan Project group leaders.[3] "The relationship between [Edith and Tilano] is hard to define," Peggy Church wrote in her book. "There was a great deal of the maternal in her care for him, though he was old enough to have been her father."[4] Edith's goddaughter remembered that her husband, Earle, "taught godfather [Tilano] to do wolf whistles—(you know the kind) and [Edith] had a particular pair of tightish jeans that always made them set up an awful howl—whistling and chirping. I know this sounds unlikely but she loved it and laughed until she was pink in the face. . . . Godfather was wonderful for her."[5] Lois Bradbury recalls how Edith would fuss over Tilano's hair braids, tying them neatly with scraps of yarn.[6] "I believe there was a great, beautiful, beautiful friendship," said Ruth Chapin, who visited Otowi.[7] Historically accurate character actress Jean Jordan, in her one-woman portrayal of Warner, handles the subject of the relationship of Edith and Tilano with humor. Jordan says to the audience, "I can't remember when Tilano moved in with me." She pauses to reflect for a moment and says in a surprised tone, "I know what you're thinking"—then she exclaims, "I am a minister's daughter!"[8]

Was the relationship of Edith and Tilano platonic? Neither of them ever said. Sue Smith, daughter of Edith's sister Mary, had the best answer: "It's nobody's business!"[9] When Françoise Ulam, wife of Polish mathematician Stanislaw, was asked about it, she laughed and exclaimed: "The million-dollar question!"[10] Some people feel that the relationship of Edith and Tilano was one of the great love stories of all time. At some point all attempts to characterize this relationship fail. There are many different kinds of love, and Tilano and Edith truly shared a unique bond—platonic or not.

One visitor who remembered Otowi at this time was Ruth Chapman, who came to visit with her best friend, Henrietta Myers, from Hanover, Pennsylvania. Ruth was nicknamed "Jennifer" and Henrietta "Peter" by their friend Larry Dawson. The name Peter stuck, as Henrietta was not fond of her birth name. Ruth remembered they had a wonderful time, even though "Miss Warner was a strict person." She recalled Edith scolding the girls for going on picnics with San Ildefonso boys, saying, "It's not fair to the Indian girls!" Both girls liked collecting rocks and loved to walk. One day Ruth returned with a handful of small stones that had caught her eye as they hiked. She proudly showed them to Tilano. He told her, "They are god stones," and opened his hand. She gave them to him.

Ruth said that Tilano usually sat on the floor, and once she admired his moccasins. He told her that he made them, took them off, and said, "Here, you can have them." She tried to refuse, but Peter was behind Tilano, shaking her head, waving her hands in the air, and silently mouthing, "Take them; take them!" Peter later told her Tilano would have been offended if she refused.[11] A pair of moccasins Tilano made for Edith are on display at the Los Alamos Historical Museum. The fine craftsmanship is evident in the careful, even stitching.

Sometimes Edith would send guests outside for Tilano to entertain and put to work. The produce from the spring-fed garden that Tilano's family had worked for generations was sold, served, and preserved. The garden was under Totavi Mesa to the south and across the highway. Lois Bradbury recalled that one day, while visiting the couple at Otowi, the cow got a leg stuck in the spring. An upset Tilano kept repeating, "Shit!"—being scolded by Edith for his choice of language—as he struggled to get the animal free and the spring flowing into the ditch again.[12]

Although the Warner household had no children, Tilano and Edith had their share of parental duties. Peter Myers and Earle Miller exchanged marriage vows at Otowi, and Tilano and Edith took on roles as active godparents to the couple. The Millers remained close and visited often, eventually building a house close to Black Mesa/ Tunyo. Peter Miller also remembered, "Juan Estevan's younger son, Rafael, lived with godmother and godfather for one winter, perhaps two—and they were always very close. Raf's mother had died when he was quite young—and as he grew into young manhood godmother stood in a mother's place for him. In those days when he stayed with them, he was in a very confused and upset state—and she used to listen to him hour after hour. She was living at Otowi then—and serving meals and her days were long and hard, but night after night . . . Raf emptied his heart out to her and went through all the twistings and turnings of adolescence. He loved her very much—and knows very well what she did for him."[13] There were also the many nephews who often spent time helping around the house and garden. If a young mother, like Peggy Church, stopped by to visit, Edith would send Tilano out with the noisy kids to chase turkeys and splash in the cold, muddy Rio. He'd tell the children stories he heard as a child. One tale was how much Tasbiyo, the giant who lived on Tunyo, loved to eat children. In just four steps the monster could be at the Rio Grande, kidnap the youngsters, and take them back to his wife to cook.[14] "Tilano loved children," Lois Bradbury said. "He was like a child."[15] Children loved him also, and so did their mothers. All the ladies who were "regulars" at the tearoom had fond memories and a favorite photo of Edith's housemate. Françoise Ulam said that when Tilano served dinner, "he always pinched the ladies."[16] "On the bottom," Kathleen Mark added. "Most men would have been slapped, but with him it seemed friendly."[17]

In a postscript to a letter to Peter, Edith remarked about "another convert to G[od]F[ather]'s charm!"[18] Everyone who knew Tilano seems to smile when they recall this remarkable man. Peter Miller wrote this memory to Peggy Church: "I remember once saying to [Edith] after I had been walking along Shumo that the mesa struck me with a terrible familiarity—in every line—and I had realized that something I knew very well in godfather [Tilano] was there in the mesa. Her smile was that glowing one as she said, 'Yes of course—they are different forms of the same thing.'"[19]

PAHN-SHADIS

I had been hoping subconsciously . . . [for] unity [in] the village. . . . It seems like the one chance for peace—here and in
the world. The "all" in their culture is so important that disunion is like a cancer. . . . This [is] a unique opportunity for
. . . unity. It will be most difficult but should be placed above
physical or personal services. . . . The disunity among Indians
is probably no greater than among the white race. The only
answer I can find is education toward awareness of universal
problems.

—*Edith Warner, letters to Peter Miller*

"*I*n those times [the 1930s] godmother used to have more social life
with the village as a whole. Later that stopped, partly because she
hadn't the strength for it, and partly because there was so much drinking among the younger people that hurtful and sad incidents were

likely to arise. But in the first days of the adobe ["guest"] house she used to give pahn-shadis [or dances] . . . for the whole village. The very first one—sort of a housewarming—must be in her journal because it was something she told so often and remembered so happily, and yet I don't remember even seeing anything she wrote about it. The whole village came—and they danced, to drum and singing, in the living room. The smaller children were put to bed in the bedrooms but there must have been quite a company of old and young in the living room. Midway through the evening, at the start of a new song, Julian asked godmother to dance. She was astonished to find no one joined them on the floor—they danced the whole song through alone. At the end Julian took a turquoise necklace out of his pocket and put it around her neck. Then Marie came forward with the little santo (that used to hang on the fireplace) and presented it to godmother. It seemed like a ceremonial moment," Peter Miller wrote in a letter to Peggy Church.[1]

"Edith was up to her eyeballs with pueblo affairs," said a friend.[2] And although Tilano took up residence at Otowi, he remained an active ceremonial and political leader at the village. Both Tilano and Edith worked long and hard to mediate and reconcile the north-south divisions at the pueblo. Some people say that the pain Edith felt over this feuding was the real reason she never finished her autobiography. "Not only would the village people have been hurt if she had written openly—but she just couldn't have done it," Edith's goddaughter wrote.[3]

Edith, who felt terrible grief about the war, took on new duties at the pueblo when the draft reached the village. In her first Christmas letter she wrote: "Early in January I was asked on the spur of the moment—yes, a woman is the head—to help in the Indian Service work at San Ildefonso. So I worked on rationing, seed orders, canning, for a small sum until August. It was good to go to the Pueblo and see the people, and I enjoyed it. There are thirteen boys in the armed services and they needed letters. The bill in Congress, threatening the Pueblos, meant more letters."

Edith and Tilano would occasionally attend parties where both

the scientists from Los Alamos and Native Americans were cele-
brating. Charlie Masters, wife of Los Alamos school superintendent
Paul, wrote, "There was born a new step—or a hundred new steps,
for each couple made its own adaptation to this strange fusion of
Amerindian rhythm and European motion. The result was a bit fan-
tastic, a bit moving. The pueblo governor moved out with Miss
Warner, an old friend of the pueblo. A scientist-guest asked the pleasure of the young Indian hostess. From then on, interracialism was
rampant. A good-neighborly time was had by all."[4]

THE HILL

"The final word has come at last and Los Alamos [Ranch School] closes Jan. 22nd with the whole place evacuated by Feb. 8th [1942]. . . . I still can't believe it and wake in the middle of the night thinking I've dreamed it. Practically the whole countryside seems [to be] leaving the mesas—and here am I. . . . My friend Oppenheimer stopped one day with some other scientists. . . . It is all very secret. . . . I feel as tho[ugh] a volcano were grumbling beneath me. . . . So keep it under whatever little gadget you wear on your head." [*Gadget* later became a code word for the atomic bomb.]
—*Edith Warner, letter to Peter Miller*

J. Robert Oppenheimer wrote: "I first knew the Pajarito Plateau in the summer of 1922, when we took a pack trip up from Frijoles and into Valle Grande. We came back to it often. In the summer of

1937 I first stopped at Edith Warner's tearoom. I was on a pack trip with my brother and sister-in-law, but came on ahead of them because one of the horses we had with us got away and I had to go after him. We had tea and chocolate cake and talk; it was my first unforgettable meeting."[1] Like Edith, Oppenheimer first visited New Mexico because of his health. He was escaping the pressures of being a gifted student and recovering from an acute case of dysentery that began a lifelong battle with digestive problems. He was preparing to enter Harvard and had rented a ranch in the Pecos Wilderness. Oppenheimer wrote a friend: "My two great loves are physics and desert country, it's a pity they can't be combined."[2] He continued, "I remember that in the summer of 1941 I brought my wife over to introduce her to Edith."[3] His wife, Kitty Harrison Oppenheimer, was a former communist whose first husband was killed fighting in the Spanish Civil War. Oppenheimer had attended some communist meetings with Kitty, but he never joined the Communist Party, as his brother Frank and sister-in-law Jackie did. At that time the Communist Party was large and well organized and Russia was the United States' ally. Attending such meetings wasn't unusual—but Oppenheimer's attendance would come back later to haunt him.

Oppenheimer and General Leslie Groves, now in charge of the Manhattan Project, stopped by Otowi for some cake in 1942. The goal of this top-secret project was, through the combined rushed efforts of several laboratories, universities, and gargantuan production facilities, to produce the first atomic bomb before Germany. Groves chose Oppenheimer to direct the activities at the heart of the project, and the two men were on their way to inspect the Los Alamos Ranch School as a possible site for their work. When they saw it, both agreed they had found the place.

Oppenheimer's first estimate was that a crew of about thirty of the best minds in nuclear engineering and theoretical physics could get the job done. Many of these scientists had fled Nazism in Europe. Several expatriated Europeans, including Nobel laureates Hans Bethe from Germany and Emilio Segre from Italy, were recruited for the project. A crew headed by Enrico Fermi, Nobel Prize winner for first splitting the atom, came from Columbia. Arthur Compton brought peers from Chicago. Others came from Berkeley, where Oppenheimer was working when Groves convinced him to head the effort. Soon this crew expanded to about six thousand young scientists, engineers, and army support staff; the average age of the workers in Los Alamos was midtwenties. These men loved working side by side with their heroes, and many later became leaders in postwar developments in their fields.

On the Hill, during their few hours off, most of the staff acted like a bunch of kids at a fraternity party. Liquor was in short supply, and anyone going to Santa Fe was expected to bring back a stash. Often laboratory 200 proof was used to spike punch. Jean Bacher, wife of bomb physics division leader Robert, wrote: "Saturday nights, the mesa rocked with a number of . . . dances and parties. Fenced in as we were, our social life was a pipeline through which we let off steam—steam with a collegiate flavor. Large dances, which often turned into binges, were popular. They were rowdy and wet parties."[4] Helen Ketola, WAC Pfc in the early days on the Hill, remembered: "The Saturday night dances would be held and then the building would have to be cleaned up for church services on Sunday morning. They could sweep up the cigarette butts and empty out the beer cans, but the stale beer odor remained. It made it almost impossible to achieve the right atmosphere for the first service when the remainders of the previous night's revelry were so apparent."[5]

Oppenheimer knew that without leave, people were likely to go stir-crazy from the stressful six-day workweeks at the isolated laboratory/military base in Los Alamos. He wanted to arrange for a few of his colleagues to go to Otowi for dinner and perhaps an occasional night on the town in Santa Fe. Groves gave in and allowed the excursions. Oppenheimer wrote, "By early 1943 we came to Los Alamos, and very early on we stopped by to talk with [Edith] and try to reassure her. We saw her regularly after that."[6]

WAR WORK

There are times I have let mere work overwhelm me. For that
I am regretful.
—*Edith Warner, postscript to Christmas Letter to Peggy Church*

*I*n 1942 Edith was beginning to have doubts if she would be able
to survive without the train. Gas was in short supply and rationed,
leaving not many tourists or locals able to drive. She was consider-
ing returning east, where there was plenty of wartime employment,
but unforeseen events enabled her to remain at her beloved Otowi.
"It was one of the Oppenheimer miracles to have arranged for his
friend Miss Warner to serve dinner to us," wrote Bernice Brode,
writer and wife of group leader Robert Brode.[1] A few couples were
allowed to enjoy the hospitality, good food, and lovely atmosphere
of the Warner house. There was always a piñon fire in the adobe
fireplace, candlelight, and the rich smells of posole (Indian corn stew)

or lamb ragout with cloves from the kitchen. "When weather permitted," Harold Agnew wrote, "we started the evening sitting outside her house . . . in the shade of some huge cottonwoods and watched the sun sink behind the mesas. When dinner was ready, Tilano called us and we sat in her dining room where Tilano served. There was no electricity and lighting was provided with oil lamps. Dinner was prepared on a large wood burning stove that had a large compartment on its side for heating water. All water had to be carried from a well from which it was drawn by bucket using a rope and pulley. The whole house had pine floors which were light gray from years of scrubbing. . . . I will always have fond memories of those special evenings with our friends and Tilano and Miss Warner at her home next to the Rio Grande."[2] Word spread, and a new adobe dining room was added in 1943 to accommodate the demand. The new tearoom was also a refuge for Edith. Peter Miller wrote, "It was a very special room having about it . . . the qualities of a kiva. Often on hot summer afternoons when . . . the log house was like an oven she would go in there for a rest and coolness. Sometimes she put a quilt down on the floor and slept for a few minutes there. . . . So complete a sanctuary."[3]

The scientists who ate in the new tearoom also noticed what a special space it was. The adobe salon at Otowi often had several Nobel Prize winners, using pseudonyms like Mr. Farmer for Enrico Fermi and Mr. Baker for Niels Bohr, for dinner. (Even after the war, these famous pioneers of theoretical physics were still called by their noms de guerre by Edith.) Due to the stress of the work and the uncomfortable temporary housing that had been thrown up in Los Alamos, it must have been a welcome diversion for the incredible staff of this international team to enjoy the "gracious but unpretentious dining" at Otowi.[4] Only the cream of the crop got to attend the dinners, and reservations were made well in advance. Harold Agnew recalls how he made reservations a minute after midnight when Edith said she had a couple of openings and would give them on a first-come basis on a certain date. He said that he wasn't the only one there at that hour with the same idea.[5] It showed status to be a regular, one of the fortunate few. Edith wore her arm out serving five or six couples from her old-fashioned kitchen, often taking two seatings nightly. Los Alamos had plenty of housewives who paid well for domestic help, so Edith and Tilano couldn't count on help from San Ildefonso. Edith charged two dollars a person and wouldn't accept tips.[6]

The dinners were outstanding. As the couples arrived, fresh corn would be put into boiling water, and she served five varieties of squash that were grown in the garden. "After the mildewed greens of the Commissary, Miss Warner's salads seemed like food for the gods," a scientist's wife remembered.[7] Fresh raspberries were served with chocolate cake for dessert.

Opinions varied on Edith's chocolate cake. Peggy Church's son Hugh said, "Edith was famous for her cake. It really was delicious. After Edith died, the recipe was never repeated successfully."[8] Lois Bradbury, Edith's best friend in Los Alamos and wife of postwar Los Alamos Laboratory director Norris Bradbury, said it was probably Betty Crocker's recipe. Lois didn't remember anything special about the cake except that "it was always there."[9] The true recipe was found in a notebook that Joan Neary, Los Alamos group leader Carson and Kathleen Mark's daughter, received as a Christmas gift from Miss Warner. Edith wanted Joan to begin a recipe collection, and the Otowi recipes for chocolate cake, chocolate frosting, spicy ginger-bread, and oatmeal bread were written on the first pages. Joan said she found the chocolate cake recipe a little dry.[10] Perhaps the trick was the fresh milk, butter, and eggs. Maybe it was the slow old wood cookstove. Surely it was the atmosphere of the house, with a large, hand-carved cottonwood bowl filled with fresh chocolate cake on the table, combined with many happy memories, that brought Edith such repute for her chocolate cake.

Robert Wilson from Princeton, one of the youngest group lead-ers in Los Alamos, first visited Otowi on horseback with Oppenheimer. On the way, they found a dead eagle and Wilson kept a few feathers. Wilson gave Tilano the feathers when they met, and an instant friend-ship was formed. Wilson was always given the honor of carving the turkey, and when his son was born, Edith and Tilano sent a collection of arrowheads. The enclosed note read: "To be a good carver you must first be a good hunter."[11] Other guests Tilano and Edith served included second laboratory director Norris Bradbury; Carson Mark, part of the British team via Canada; Phillip Morrison, Oppenheimer's brilliant student; Sam Allison, physicist from Chicago; Edward Teller, Hungarian refugee and self-proclaimed "father of the hydrogen bomb"; and Stanislaw Ulam, Polish mathematician.

Edith's war work was feeding hungry scientists,[12] but unlike Mabel Dodge Luhan, who invited exceptional people to her house in Taos, Edith never sought this company. Circumstances created this meeting place of extraordinary minds. Edith wasn't supposed to know what the scientists were doing on the Hill; even the scientists' wives weren't told what kept their husbands busy days, nights, and weekends. "Edith didn't approve of what we were doing," Lois Bradbury said.[13] "The world situation caused her grief," experimental physicist John Manley's wife, Kay, recalls.[14] Project historian David Hawkins wrote, "She never joined in the conversation before or after dinner."[15] Philip Morrison wrote to Edith, "It would have been easy for you to reject our problem. You could have drawn away from the Hill people and their concerns."[16] David Hawkins agreed: "The smile comes back to me more often than other recollections of Edith Warner."[17]

Danish Nobelist/statesman Niels Bohr was one scientist who Peter Miller remembers left a deep impression on Edith: "They recognized each other's qualities instantly. She always felt that she had something to learn from him—and I remember her saying that she felt for a long time that he might give her a magic word . . . and then smiling she said—'But now I know there is no magic word—or need for any.'" Peter continued, "She wrote of how Oppenheimer had come down for a day's rest—and after he'd spent the afternoon in the adobe house came over to the kitchen for supper and talked and talked. She admired him too—but not in quite the same way as Bohr—not as someone from whom she could learn. She was several times tempted to write to Bohr asking, 'What is it you can say to me?' She always hoped for another meeting with him."[18] Bohr said, "[Edith] had an intuitive understanding which was a bond between us."[19]

Edith's house was closed to the public. In contrast to the collegiate party atmosphere up on the Hill, at the tearoom everyone behaved themselves, and there was no drinking. Edith probably forbade alcohol because she wanted Tilano to remain sober. Usually the groups would carpool, bringing along a bottle for the hair-raising ride down the two steep hills from the mesa and saving what was left under the seat for the drive home.[20] The men would talk quietly, and the women would decide who got the produce for sale from the garden. Edith's warm kitchen became a safety valve that helped keep the pressure cooker up on the Hill from blowing. But then it did blow.

THE GADGET

We learn so slowly and how can the world survive many wars?
                              —*Edith Warner, letter to Peter Miller*

*E*dith and Tilano were thankful for some peace in early 1945. After an exodus of trucks from Los Alamos, the traffic had let up, and no blasts came from the Hill. The men were down south, preparing ground zero in the desert at White Sands near Alamogordo, New Mexico. Oppenheimer named the test site for the atomic bomb Trinity,[1] but the early Spanish explorers had aptly called this route Jornada del Muerto—Journey of Death.

Edith Warner had more of a hunch than most about what had been going on up on the Hill, but someone of such a peaceful, quiet nature didn't want to probe. She wrote in a Christmas letter: "I had not known what was being done up there, though in the beginning I had suspected atomic research."

Even the scientists were unclear about the true power of the atom and the Pandora's box they were opening. No one knew if the Gadget was going to be a dud, a little bigger bang than conventional bombs of the era, or Armageddon. Before sunrise on July 16, 1945, the crew killed time waiting for the Trinity test by placing bets on what the power of the plutonium bomb's blast would be. The wagers ranged from zero to thirty kilotons of TNT. Robert Oppenheimer went low at three thousand pounds—a far cry short of the blast they were about to witness of two hundred tons of TNT. The waiting already had the scientists sweating bullets while Fermi further agitated the tense situation by reminding everyone that the bomb could ignite the atmosphere, ending all life on earth. He had already calculated that the chances were one in thirty that New Mexico would be destroyed and was taking side bets that this would happen. Finally, at 5:29 A.M., the world's first man-made plutonium Big Bang lit up the night sky, creating a crater four hundred yards wide. Less than a month later, when the world's second plutonium bomb, "Fat Man" (named for Winston Churchill because of its five-foot girth), was dropped on Nagasaki, there were an estimated sixty-four thousand casualties. Three days before, on August 6, 1945, when Hiroshima was slammed by "Little Boy," the first, untested ten-foot-long uranium bomb weighing nine thousand pounds, an estimated 135,000 casualties resulted. This was a lot more than Oppenheimer had bargained for. Edith Warner wrote in her third Christmas letter: "The climax came on that August day when the report of the atomic bomb flashed around the world. It seemed fitting that it was Kitty Oppenheimer who, coming for vegetables, brought the news. . . . The war is over. Peace is still to be secured. The scientists know that they cannot go back to their laboratories leaving atomic energy in the hands of the armed forces or the statesmen. Nor can I concern myself only with my kitchen, for I, too, am one of the people."

AFTERMATH

> Soldiers and sailors had returned from Europe and Japan to
> lay aside uniforms and wear again ceremonial kirtles and
> moccasins. Could the habits of war be so easily discarded?
> —*Edith Warner, fourth Christmas Report*

*E*dith Warner celebrated the end of the war with the rest of the
nation. She especially looked forward to seeing the Native American
soldiers return. Bernice Brode wrote: "Like us, she thought the bomb
need never be used again, now that its devastation was known to the
world, and that it might play a role in ending wars for all time."[1]

The big change from overseas duty back to pueblo life was
difficult for the Native Americans. They had been allowed to drink
openly in the military, and when they returned, many of the Indian
veterans refused to undergo the traditional purification ceremonies
needed to cleanse the spirit. Edith and Tilano were concerned that

the old ways were being lost. The end of the war brought joy with the return of the boys but also caused deep concern and heavy hearts at Otowi.[2]

Edith had refused to visit Los Alamos after the "gate," a shack with MPs, was erected—she would politely decline invitations, saying it was better that she just hear about the changes. She finally made the journey up the Hill in 1945 when the secret was out.[3] Sometimes she would visit with friends like Norris and Lois Bradbury, but as Kathleen Mark said, "She never stayed long."[4]

Los Alamos faced an uncertain future. Now that the mission was accomplished, many of the original crew were being lured away to posts in business and universities with good salaries and comfortable housing. Other young scientists had more work to complete at universities. Oppenheimer wanted to return to academic life at Cal Tech in Pasadena. On October 16, 1945, Fuller Lodge was decked out for the occasion of the U.S. Army honoring the work at Los Alamos. In his speech Oppenheimer said: "If atomic bombs are to be added to the arsenals of a warring world, or to the arsenals of nations preparing for war, then the time will come when mankind will curse the names of Los Alamos and Hiroshima. The people of the world must unite, or they will perish."[5] For a while Oppenheimer was a national hero and celebrity. His knowledge and charisma made him a favorite among journalists eager to speculate about America's atomic future. This didn't last long in the Cold War environment that was gripping America. The civilian Atomic Energy Commission, which Oppenheimer had helped create and once chaired, decided he was a "security risk,"[6] and for thirteen years he was under heavy surveillance for making statements like: "The physicists have known sin; and this is a knowledge which they cannot lose."[7]

Norris Bradbury was chosen to succeed Oppenheimer as head of the lab. He was left with chaos and unanswered questions. What was the future of atomic energy? Would some of the staff stay? What were the goals of the new Los Alamos? He had to address many other questions about budget, funding, and housing. Groves assured the lab workers that the mission was not over. Plans were already brewing to develop a hydrogen bomb with a thousand times more bang than the existing atomic bombs. Oppenheimer openly opposed the idea of the "super" on technological, political, and moral grounds. He admitted that it was "technically sweet"—but so was Eve's apple.[8] Bradbury thought that he had about three years to develop a bomb that would "insure peace," and he called for more tests.[9] He later admitted to Bill Beyer, a mathematician who had worked at the lab for forty-four years, "I spent my whole life working on something nobody could use."[10]

THE NEW HOUSE

> To those who made a strong foundation, a tight roof and
> smooth walls for a house on the side of a mesa; who endured
> heat, blisters, sore muscles and came again; who gave brain,
> brawn and moral support— . . . I hope you will feel that it
> is your house, too, and use it. The latch string is always out.
> —*Edith Warner, letter to Lois Bradbury*

As the Hill kept growing, a new, wider bridge was needed for the
increased traffic. Edith and Tilano were forced to move. Bernice
Brode wrote: "I suggested she was one of the victims of the new
atomic age, and Tilano nodded his head, as he turned his thumb
toward the Hill on the plateau.'Cars go up and cars go down—every-
body full of talk-talk-talk.'"[1] Scientists and Native Americans worked
side by side to build a new house across the road, close to the old
garden. Some say that the pueblo had to rebuild the "Sunday work"

on Monday.[2] The builders from the pueblo certainly understood the techniques of traditional New Mexico construction best, but the scientists supplied much sweat and materials to construct the beautiful house that was completed in 1947. It still stands. Peter Miller said, "The house at Totavi, the new house, seemed almost more than the other to be 'in the curve beneath the wave'—and [Edith] loved it for that."[3] Still, it was difficult for Tilano and Edith to pull up roots from the old pitched roof wood-and-adobe casa that meant so much to many people—especially themselves.

Edith began her unfinished autobiography with the building of the new house. Edith's sister Velma suggested to Peggy Church that her biography of Edith "would be stronger if you started at the other end and then had a flashback to earlier days. The last three years were the strongest ones it seems to me and hence the result of the earlier period."[4]

FLYING SOUTH

On grey days like this I so often think of wild geese flying
south.... Now above, now below, the broken mesa rim they
flew, with never a moment of hesitation, with always the
memory of warm, plentiful feeding grounds, and an old trail
to them. Where the river turns again, they rose above the
mesa, and my last glimpse was that swaying line against
lighter clouds—winging southward. Death could be like
that.

—*Edith Warner, journal entry, February 7, 1935*

When Edith was diagnosed with cancer, she went to the Illinois
Masonic Hospital in Chicago, and on January 25, 1951, she had an
unsuccessful operation.[1] Ironically, the doctors referred her for experimental radiation treatments at "an obscure place called Los Alamos."[2]
She gave it a try, but unfortunately the new therapy had no positive

results. Edith's doctors recommended further surgery. She refused. By then Edith had given up solid food completely.

Velma wrote: "She is taking it the way she lived—gallantly."[3] "In spite of her pain, I have never known anyone so relaxed and content in the face of death," a visiting health-care provider said.[4] Robert Oppenheimer saw Edith "for the last time the summer before her death, after she had moved to the new house."[5] Lois Bradbury said that Edith's friends from the pueblo came for a last visit to say good-bye and Edith gave each one a book.[6] "Almost all the village people came before she died. To hear those silent ones talk was an experience in itself. Their words were powerful. I shall never forget it," Edith's sister Velma wrote.[7] Peter Miller remembered Edith telling her, "Nothing is ever lost," and before Edith died, she said to her god-daughter, "The village people know now that the gods have accepted me."[8] Edith's friend, Sarah McComb, said, "[Edith] showed us how to live. Now she is showing us all how to die."[9]

Lois Bradbury was by her side when Edith Warner died at the new house on May 4, 1951.[10] That same night, according to custom, Tilano arranged a Catholic ceremony, private funeral services were held, and she was buried near the new house. San Ildefonso mourned for four days. Her unmarked grave is on San Ildefonso property close to her beloved Rio Grande.

Maria's son Adam and his wife, Santanya, came to stay with Tilano at the new house. Bernice Brode observed that Edith's fastidiously tidy housekeeping "gave way to more casual attention to house and garden. The little valley near the Rio Grande will never be the same again, because no one could follow in the footsteps of the meticulous, gentle lady from Philadelphia, with the artist's love for every wild bloom and colored rock and changing tree in the desert of New Mexico."[11]

One of the last things Edith took care of was to mail order enough jeans from Montgomery Ward to last Tilano two years.[12] He died almost two years later.

OTOWI TODAY

Here, bounded by railroad and river, with the road not far
from its door, the little house watched the years pass. . . .
              —*Edith Warner, autobiography*

*A*s I drove out to Otowi, I wondered what Edith would think of
what's left of her old place. It's been about fifty years since she built
the new house under Totavi. The superhighway has added another
couple of lanes since the original expansion that brought the need
to move. The guest house and tearoom are still there, but nothing's
left of her original house. There was a For Rent sign on the open
gate, so I pulled in. A truck, with a San Ildefonso man inside, looking straight ahead, was parked in the driveway. I wandered up, wondering if he noticed me. "I saw the sign," I said. "How much?"

"Five hundred dollars a month," he answered, still looking straight
ahead. "First, last, and a year's lease. Want to see it?"

"Yeah, I might be interested," I said.

As he unlocked the door he said, "*This* is where the atomic bomb was made—not up there," pointing toward the Hill.

I laughed. There's indoor plumbing in the house now, and a propane heater has replaced Tilano's fireplace as the main source of heat. It was bitterly cold as he showed me around. "Could use some fixing up," I said. We were soon back out in the bright winter sun, where I found a warm spot against a south wall. Under Edith's favorite cottonwood was a pile of aluminum cans, and the man tossed another one on top. "What's that?" I asked, pointing at the tearoom.

As he unlocked it he answered, "Storage—I was going to fix it up. Do you work on the Hill?"

"No, I'm a teacher in Pojoaque," I answered.

"I went to school there," he said, "played football. I still have a trophy. We were state champs, the best! Now they can't win a game. For you, I'll rent it for four hundred dollars."

Inside the tearoom were a couple of stacks of bags of hardened cement and lots of big spiders. I asked, "What if I wanted to open it up as a tearoom again?"

"Six hundred dollars a month!" He laughed and said, "What was her name—that lady?"

"Edith Warner," I answered, "did you know her?"

"I used to work in the garden over there with Tilano." He pointed across the highway as we walked over to the adobe house by the river. "This was his house. That's where the *atomic bomb* was made," he repeated, pointing at the tearoom.

"I know the story." I chuckled.

"How do you know so much?" he asked. "Did you read that book?"

"Yeah," I answered, "both of them."

I started telling him about Edith's writing, but he interrupted and said, "Smart lady—but there's been too much written already."

I agreed and asked if I could look around. I walked down by the old bridge, which still sits quietly by the huge highway that crosses the Rio Grande today. Few people even look as the cars rush by. It's almost impossible to hear the song of the river anymore with all the noise from the traffic.

I thought how San Ildefonso and Los Alamos haven't changed much over the years, but Otowi has. Edith probably would be happy to know that San Ildefonso is one of the few pueblos that haven't opened up a casino yet. The pueblo keeps their traditions alive, and their art, especially the pottery, is still the main source of revenue. She probably would be disappointed but not surprised to know that the mission of Los Alamos is still the same as it was when she hosted the men and women who began the atomic era. The arms race ended in 1989, but the Hill is still growing. Los Alamos has started making plutonium "pits" for atomic bombs again, something it hasn't done since the first three were made while Edith lived by the river.[1] The inertia that kept work on the Hill going after Germany's defeat, after the bombing of Japan, and after the Cold War ended keeps it going today. The dream that Edith Warner, Niels Bohr, and J. Robert Oppenheimer all had of an international sharing and control of this new knowledge of the atom became a nightmare—the 1970s had produced approximately a hundred thousand bombs in the United States and the Soviet Union.[2]

After a while I asked if I could go inside and take one last look at the adobe. I walked over to the fireplace Tilano built and thought about how Edith loved gathering wood. Harnessing the energy of a renewable resource for fire was enough for her. She had written in the 1946 Christmas letter:

> It was time to prepare for winter and we went happily up on the Plateau to gather pineknots for the fireplaces. Now, as I recall the feel of warm sunshine, the smell of pine needles, the sound of the wind high in the trees, the peace of the little canyon, I find myself contrasting that fuel getting with the mining of coal.
>
> Such mental questioning and awareness of the world prompted formation of a small discussion group here in the valley. It is an attempt to increase our share of public opin-

ion by pooling our information and clarifying our reactions. Most of us find it an incentive and a mental stimulus. Perhaps, too, it is a beginning of community awareness. We, all Anglos, are the newcomers in a valley long inhabited by Spanish Americans and Indians—a small-scale world. My hope is a real community group.

As I drove home I started dreaming about how great it would be to revive the tearoom and try to restore that special place. I called Hedy Dunn, director of the Los Alamos Historic Foundation, and asked what she thought about such a notion. "You're full of ideas, aren't you?" she replied. There is no historic landmark sign or any indication that the property was once a favorite destination of locals and tourists for some of that famous Otowi chocolate loaf cake and interesting conversation. I realized I could never revive that place properly—no one could. Even Edith and Tilano left it behind half a century ago. Then I started wondering why I ever even took on this project. A few years ago, when I visited the Los Alamos Historic Foundation and asked if they had a copy of Edith Warner's unfinished autobiography, I had no idea what I was getting into. I just had a passion to find anything Edith Warner wrote. I didn't choose to do this book—it chose me.

As the atomic age is passing and a new millennium begins, Edith's deceptively simple wishes for true community and peace in the world are still as vital and viable as they were when she wrote about them. Her intuition and vision were just ahead of her time. Perhaps with the new century, her wishes will come true.

PART II

Selected Writings of Edith Warner

The following text, Edith Warner's unfinished autobiography, is reprinted the way Edith left it in about 1948 to 1949. She wrote a slightly shorter version of chapter 2, but I've decided to use the longer one. Except for a few minor changes, the editing job is hers.

IN THE SHADOW OF LOS ALAMOS

ℐtatement of Purpose

Repeatedly it has been brought to my attention that the house at Otowi Bridge, where I lived for twenty years, was unique in quality as well as location. It stood between the indigenous Pueblo culture and the new transplanted Anglo culture, represented recently by the new Los Alamos and the atomic era. Its quality was compounded of both cultures and influenced some at least who came in contact with it. To a certain extent this quality has been felt in the five Christmas letters, so that there have been requests for more of the story.

My purpose is to tell the story of the house against a background of changing seasons and Pueblo activities; to show the relationship of individual Indians with the house and their influence upon its growth; to weave through the record the intangible quality of the house. I am not an ethnologist and in no sense present any material as scientific information. The Indians described are friends. Because I respect Pueblo reticence there are some things which cannot be written, but I do not think the omission affects the whole.

Since I must earn a living, I have been able to relive and record only the first few months of the story. The way it unfolds and what hidden meanings arise I have no way of knowing now. Recently certain aspects have begun to clarify and the whole to take on some form, but it is still a matter of going back into the years—almost feeling with my hands for what became part of the structure. I think it has to be brought out into the open and put into words before true evaluation is possible. For this, time is necessary.

$\mathcal{F}$oreword

Lunch under the big cottonwoods in the meadow was to be late on that day in early July. Clouds had gathered in the noon heat, but this time, strangely enough, they had been watched with apprehension rather than hope, in spite of the shriveling corn, for the

kitchen roof of the new house across the arroyo had to be laid before the rain came.

The roof was on and with a feeling of achievement, as well as relief, men and women rested in the shade. Temporarily the jug of ice water had slaked their thirst. Ragout, homemade bread, garden lettuce, and chocolate cake had satisfied their hunger and renewed their strength for more hours of work on this house—a house being made by many hands and hearts.

Against one old tree leaned Tilano, who, like this cottonwood, had watched roads and bridges change the Pueblo land over a span of seven decades. The years had lined his face and the tree trunk, but the long braids bound with azure yarn were still black, and his eyes twinkled as easily as the leaves above him danced in the gentlest breeze. Between

the spreading, water-searching roots of a neighboring tree, another builder rested. With fewer fields under cultivation in this year of little rain, Tony had turned his agile hands to the shaping of a house drawn upward from the mesa-side. He was of the next generation likely to be the last to tie long hair in a chongo, to wear moccasins by choice.

Scattered on the grass between these two Pueblo Indians were men and women from Los Alamos—men who had participated in the birth of the atomic bomb on a well-guarded mesa, women who had shared the long months of tension before the first bomb was exploded at Trinity. Their children slowly finished lunch, happily tired after a morning of play in the arroyo's trickle of water.

The last cup of coffee had been poured, and I sat down for a conference with these builders in adobe. What had started as a barn-raising, an act of neighborliness in which the foundation was laid, had become another tradition in this land of many traditions. Each weekend about fifteen people came down into the valley from Los Alamos to mix mud, make adobe bricks, peel pine saplings, lay roofs, plaster walls. This had become a group project of many people. Some, who could not build, made possible the material for the builders. Many helped unknowingly, their memory of the old house creating the impetus which made possible the new one. This new house was an outgrowth and a result of that old house at

Otowi Bridge past which now streams the heavy traffic to Los Alamos.

Because the old house had come to have meaning for those who knew it, I have tried to record the years of its growing, and the way in which the Atomic Era brought those years to a close.

CHAPTER 1

$\mathcal{T}$his is a story of a house that stood detached, between the Pueblo Indian world and the Anglo—a house destined to play a part in the lives of the men and women who brought into being the atomic bomb.

In 1928 it was an ugly little frame house with a peaked roof that was conspicuous in a land where adobe flat-roofed houses, blending with their mother earth, are almost invisible. Its boards, laid horizontally, were painted a drab tan, and the roofing-paper top showed the strength of New Mexico sunshine. Its sole adornment was a large Coca-Cola sign on the small front porch, beside which a gasoline pump stood forlornly.

The only trees on the sandy acre were a few junipers, although down along the riverbank young cottonwoods struggled to live. Spice bush and a prickly pear cactus here and there anchored some of the sand when spring winds blew. But the well-house, nearby, its timber weathered to a soft gray, had charm.

About two hundred steps west of the porch were the tracks of the Denver and Rio Grande narrow gauge railroad. Beside it was an old boxcar station painted the same color as the house and marked OTOWI. The Rio Grande River was parallel to the railroad and, south of the house, was crossed by a suspension bridge known as Otowi Bridge. The washboard gravel road formed a link between Santa Fe, twenty-three miles to the southeast, and the mountains to the west. Here, bounded by railroad and river, with the road not far from its door, the little house watched the years pass and these boundaries change.

Originally two rooms of the house had been part of a logging camp on the south side of the road. Some of the San Ildefonso Indians had hauled logs for the railroad ties from the mountains to Otowi Station, sleeping at the camp during the week to avoid the river crossing. Always they spoke of the site as Campito, and even now their children, wanting to visit the house at the bridge, say, "Take us to Campito."

When logging operations ceased, Shorty, a Portuguese who had worked there, decided to obtain the house for his own use and move it to a better location across the railroad. Since all the land was part of the San Ildefonso reservation, he persuaded one of the Indians to ask the Pueblo Council for the use of this acre, and then to rent it to him. Having accomplished this, he moved the house, which barely missed being struck by the southbound train when one of the rollers got caught in the track. After adding a room and digging a well, Shorty opened a store which offered the few passersby soft drinks, tobacco, and canned food. The quantity of broken bottles around the house may have indicated an additional source of income, and, since those were Prohibition years, may have been the reason for his departure.

However, the main excuse for Shorty's living near the station was Los Alamos Ranch School, a private school for boys on Los Alamos Mesa, ten miles west of Otowi Station and two thousand feet above it. All mail and supplies for the school, which had its own commissary, dairy herd, and horses, were shipped to Otowi by train and trucked up the steep hill to the mesa. The school truck made only three trips weekly, which necessitated someone living nearby to take care of the freight.

When Shorty left the little house by the river, Adam, a young Indian, fell heir to the job. Adam's father and mother, Julian and Maria Martinez of San Ildefonso Pueblo, bought the house from Shorty, since it stood on their land, and Adam, adding a fourth room, took his wife to live there. But it was lonely in spite of two trains a day, and they returned to the Pueblo. This left the little house unoccupied, the freight unprotected, and soon led to a crisis.

Mr. Connell, director of the school, was an Irishman who usually obtained his objective, whether that was a boy for the school or a lawn in a dry land. He went to Santa Fe determined to find a responsible man who would stay at Otowi Station, but unfortunately no one wanted to live way out there with the only inducement an assured income of twenty-five dollars monthly. During the evening he chanced to see me at La Fonda, in Santa Fe. I also was determined—determined to find some way of earning a living in New Mexico. That day I had eliminated the last known possibility.

I had come first to New Mexico in the fall of 1922, when a wise diagnostician, finding no physical cause for a persistent illness, suggested an outdoor life without responsibility. Perhaps the war and post-war years had been too strenuous. Perhaps subconsciously I was

rebelling against the speed of city living. Perhaps unknown forces were changing the pattern of my life, for I chose to follow an inexplicable urge which led me to the Southwest. A year in the canyons and mountains of New Mexico followed—a year of walking and riding, of resting on the warm earth—and I knew that I could live happily nowhere else. When of necessity I went away, it was with the determination of returning.

In September of 1927 I was asked to spend the winter tutoring a small boy at Anchor Ranch, three miles south of Los Alamos. After I came back to New Mexico, the next step was to find a way to remain. My ideas of how I might earn a living in a sparsely inhabited country had been numerous but not practical for an unmarried woman of thirty-five with no capital. Certainly those ideas had not included taking care of freight or selling gasoline and Coca-Cola in an ugly frame house at Otowi Bridge. And this was just what Mr. Connell, in desperation, suggested I do.

"You want to stay in this country, don't you?" he asked.

"Yes, but—"

"You can rent the house from Maria and Julian for very little. Tell them I sent you. Get Adam to go over from the Pueblo to unload the freight—and see that he gets there on time. With you living there, no one will attempt theft. What we pay you should cover rent and Adam's wages. How soon can you arrange to take over?"

A decision had to be made at once. There was no point in trying to consult my family who, never having been in New Mexico, had no conception of the circumstances. They had helped me as long as they could, and then had become resigned to my solving the problem alone. They must have had faith in the Lord—and perhaps some in me, for they had never put any obstacles in my way.

Return east I would not. Waiting for another opportunity was too much of a gamble. His offer would at least tide me over until I could find a better solution. I decided to try it.

The next day I went to San Ildefonso and arranged with Maria and Julian to rent the house, subject to the approval of the Pueblo Council and the Indian Service. Their son, Adam, agreed to do the actual freight work plus my wood-chopping. So with many doubts and fears, I cast my lot with this house of dubious antecedents.

Atilano

CHAPTER 2

$\mathcal{S}$pring was late in 1928, and when I came to the house by the river on that first day of May, not a shiny green leaf brightened the drabness. My heart sank as I walked through its rooms and saw the faded wallboard on ceilings, rough, board floors with cracks, and tin-covered knotholes. The corner room of the L-shaped house had no ceiling, save its roof of weather-stained boards, only two small windows, and an old stove. In the room Shorty had used as a store were my trunks, boxes of books, a barrel of dishes, two Montgomery-Ward folding iron beds, and four chairs.

Fortunately, there was work to be done, and I started on the middle room, which was to be the kitchen. A ticking clock and a pot of ivy on a high window sill, a bright Navajo rug on the floor, and a teakettle on the stove were like magic. Doubts began to be overshadowed by excitement. Boxes became a table and cupboard. A soft-colored Chimayo blanket turned one of the narrow beds into a couch, and to my delight, one room had become habitable. A pattern for temporary living had been established, and now my awareness began to reach outside the house.

The afternoon train had whistled shrilly for the crossing and rattled south without stopping. Now and then a car passed over the bridge. The only neighbors, Spanish-Americans whom I had never seen, lived on the other side of the river and a mile away. I was alone—utterly alone.

After supper I sat on the steps of the kitchen door, which faced south. The cottonwoods near the river had no leaves to soften their dark outline save the fluttery dry ones that had clung to the branches all through the winter. The only sound was that made by the rushing Rio Grande swollen by melting snow; but as I listened there seemed more than the noise of much water. Suddenly, in that hour before the twilight, I became aware of the song of the river. Always, even when there is little water, the song comes from below the bridge where the rocks pit their strength against the river. The Indians call it Po-sah-con-gay, "the place where the water makes a noise." On many a night in the twenty years that followed, I was to stand at the kitchen door listening as the river made of its noise a song—a song that became the melody of living.

Gradually, my eyes rose to the two mesas which form a canyon for the river. In the evening light they seemed to have been drawn upward from the earth by a giant hand, to curve against the sky as far as the eye could see. From their flat tops the house must have looked like a matchbox, and I in its doorway, an ant. With their crown of dark rock they were awesome but not frightening. Rather they were like two massive ancient ones who had seen much. Their firm anchorage and their great age were comforting. As the evening star sank beneath the rim of the western mesa, I began to feel that they had accepted me, and to suspect that if I had endurance, life in the little house could be satisfying.

The next day was cold and rainy. Hearing horses' hoofbeats on the bridge, I looked out to see two young Indians entering the yard. One of them was Adam. I had seen him only twice before, but he was as welcome as an old friend. A shy smile answered my loneliness, as he said, "This is my cousin, Richard. I brought him to help me unload the oats. The trainmen want to take the empty car tomorrow."

I shook hands with Richard, saying, "I'm sorry you have to do it in the rain. Come to the house when you finish and get warm."

As they walked toward the railroad, I turned eagerly to prepare tea for my first guests. Very soon I learned to keep a pot of coffee ready for visitors, but when they came in, wet and cold, an hour later, they drank the hot tea as though it were their favorite beverage. We laughed together when Richard, accepting more oatmeal cookies, looked at the box around which we sat and said, "This is a good table you made." That broke the restraint and, glancing around the room, Adam turned to me and said, "Already it is different, it looks nice."

As we discussed the weather and the freight arrangements, I saw that these cousins were alike only in their sense of humor and the way in which they wore their hair. Even then many younger Indians continued to keep their hair cut short after they had finished school. But Adam and Richard let theirs grow, parted it in the middle, tied it with yarn, and brought the braids forward to hang in front of the shoulder. Adam was short and compactly built, while Richard was lean and loose-limbed, with the eyes of a mystic.

Not being accustomed to women who live alone, they probably thought I was queer, but they were too polite to intimate it. Naturally there was curiosity, and perhaps some concern, for as they left, Adam asked, "You aren't afraid here by yourself?"

"Not much," I assured him, "and soon a friend is coming to stay with me."

As darkness shut out my guarding mesas, I now had to face this thing called being afraid. Eliminating the elements, which are in a category apart, there were man and insecurity to fear. Having so little of material worth, and a locked door, I had no reason to fear man; and even those who have security must be concerned lest they lose it. That night, at last, only a vague uneasiness remained, and I slept soundly.

Just what I should have done in case robbery of the station were attempted, I never knew. When some weeks later, I was given a revolver, the grapevine carried the word through the valley that loiterers after dark would be asked no questions. One night I awoke suddenly with the uneasy feeling that someone was near. My impression was so vivid that I jumped out of bed and reached for the gun. Clouds partially covered the moon, but there was enough light for me to see a man run from the screen door toward the bridge where he had tied his horse. I opened the door and clutched the gun with trembling hands. As I fired a shot into the air, horse and rider galloped away, and I was again alone in the stillness of the night.

Obviously the situation called for a dog, and some of the precious dollars had been spent for an Airedale pup called Paddy. A mongrel dog from the Pueblo would have been better. Paddy did not survive the summer, and after I had lost her, it was a long while before I tried another. Eventually, there followed a succession of friendly dogs. Without a fenced yard, a good watchdog was impracticable, so each dog in his turn was "a company," but never a guardian.

At the end of the first week, Lottie, a friend from the East, came to help me get the house in shape. She was older and more experienced, and had a good sense of humor, which offset her tendency to be somewhat dour. She liked the country and the Pueblo people, and they liked her. Her help and advice carried me through that summer of experimentation and adjustment. I had hoped she might stay on, but before the summer ended we realized that this was not feasible. Fortunately for both of us, she could practice her profession of nursing in Santa Fe and come out to the house between cases.

As soon as Lottie became adjusted to the altitude, we began to work on the house, a job which was easier for two women to plan than to accomplish. We needed a man to build cupboards and closets, to put windows in the corner room. "Perhaps Ignacio can tell us of someone," I suggested. "Let's walk over to the Pueblo."

As we crossed the bridge and walked along the road toward the Pueblo, I recalled the first time I had gone to San Ildefonso with John Boyd. On that day, when the old topless Ford had achieved a hill, the valley lay before us like a magic land—a sight I had never forgotten. Then it had been a golden land under the afternoon sun with clouds casting their shadows as they moved like great birds in a blue sky. Now the cottonwoods along the river had green leaves, and, in Adam's field beside the road, spring wheat was pushing up through the brown earth. Cholla cactus bordering the shortcut was forming buds that would open into cerise blossoms in June, and chamisa was changing its winter gray for a soft new green. After we passed the wide arroyo, the road wound between low hills and fields where fragrant wild plum thickets bloomed along the acequias. Ahead we could see smoke rising

from chimneys in the Pueblo, and beyond it, the Black Mesa standing alone beside the river.

The people of San Ildefonso still build adobe houses around a plaza as their ancestors did when the Pueblo was established on the east side of the river in the sixteenth century. Houses have varied and changed as have their builders; but the round kiva in the south plaza and the great cottonwood in the north plaza remain, marked only by the years and the elements.

It was during my first New Mexico winter, spent at the guest ranch in Frijoles Canyon, that my host, John Boyd, had brought me to San Ildefonso. After the Christmas candy was distributed, we went to see Ignacio Aguilar, and I was welcomed because I came with his friend, Mr. Boyd. This tall, lean, mustached Hoosier with the easy manner and twinkling eyes liked people, and especially those who appreciated his many tales. But most of all he liked his Indian friends who laughed when he teased them, and asked his advice when they were perplexed. On that cold day we sat in front of the fireplace while the men talked of the coming feast day and I looked with diffidence at the long room with its white walls and beamed ceiling. On a pole suspended from the vigas were arranged the family's ceremonial garments, striped blankets, and buckskin leggings. Holy pictures and a rosary hung on the wall. There was little furniture. A long roll against one wall served as seat by day and, when spread out, as bed by night. Several straight chairs and homemade stools [were] by the corner fireplace where a stick or two of piñon stood upright, and made a surprising amount of heat. I was enjoying the spaciousness and dignity of this uncluttered room when I heard Mr. Boyd say, "I want to bring this easterner down for San Ildefonso day. Do you think we might stay here?"

"My house is yours," Ignacio answered, even though he knew how many visiting Indians and Spanish-Americans came down for the feast.

He meant what he said, this little man with eyes that were both kind and shrewd. His iron-gray hair was cut so that bangs and long side-locks framed his wrinkled face with the rest drawn back, doubled up, and tied at the neck. Besides being a good farmer, Ignacio could tan a deerskin so that it was soft and white for moccasins. The gnarled brown hands resting on his knees had scattered wheat for many plantings and heaped the corn for many huskings. All the trails, as well as the plants of mountain and mesa, were known to him. Ignacio had been trained in the ritual of the Mass and served the priest throughout his life; but in addition, there had been handed down to him by word of mouth the vast and ancient knowledge essential for the position he held in the Pueblo.

From that day I had been welcomed at the Aguilar home whenever there was occasion to go to the Pueblo. Now, I turned to Ignacio naturally, knowing he would help if he could.

Children were playing outside the house as we drew near, and Florencita, a six-year-old whom I had known first as a toddler, came to meet us. She had grown to look like her mother, Rosalie, with big eyes as black as the bangs above them, and a broad smile. Florencita's English was limited to "hello," "goodbye," "candy," and "thank you," but that was no obstacle to the games we often played together. When she heard us, Rosalie came to the door and with a smile said, "Oh, you came at last. We've been looking for you. Come in."

Rosalie had come from Picuris, one of the northern pueblos, when she married Ignacio's son, Joe. She had learned to speak Tewa, the language of San Ildefonso, and fitted into family and village life as though she had been born there. Susana, her mother-in-law, had taught her to make pottery, and the two women now sat on low stools by the fireplace polishing bowls that had been shaped earlier in the week.

Probably it was because she understood no English that Susana seemed shy and withdrawn as we chatted. Our attempts at conversation were seldom very successful; but this gentle woman found other ways of communicating, and I have treasured the expression in her eyes as much as the gifts she placed in my hands.

When I asked for Ignacio, Rosalie consulted Susana. Then she said, "My father and Joe are in the fields down near the river, but they will come soon. My mother says you must wait."

I went to sit on the doorstep with the children. In this country there is need to sit quietly now and then—to look, to listen, to feel. Even the children were quiet as they ate tortillas. As I watched the lengthening shadow of the round kiva, I was thinking of another summer day when I had ridden down to the Pueblo from the mountains.

Each detail of that earlier trip was etched clearly on my memory, and now again, I relived that vital experience. After supper Ignacio had placed chairs outside the doorway in the cool of the evening. Relaxing after the long day's ride, I had rested my head against the adobe wall of the house and was watching the afterglow touch the kiva, the carved mesas across the river, the big mesa to the south. As it faded and the evening star shone above the western mesa's curving rim, the singing of an age-old song came from the north plaza where the Pueblo boys had gathered under the big cottonwood. Then Ignacio's voice roused me and I listened to the story of Avanyu.

He began by asking if I had seen the pottery bowl Susana had fired that day. "Did you see what was painted on it? That is Avanyu, the plumed serpent. I will tell you about him. He lives many miles away in a deep lake. Sometimes he does not come for many months. We plant corn and wheat, but the ground is hard. They come up and grow a little, but if no rain comes, they die. We have no atole, no bread for winter. Then we pray and dance—all the men and women

and children. We dance all day and maybe all night. And when we dance, if our hearts are right, he comes. No matter if the ice be that thick," and Ignacio held his hand several feet above the ground, "he breaks through and comes in the black clouds."

Little did I think, as the spell of his words ended, that the years would bring me to live a few miles from the Pueblo, where the people danced for rain. There was no inkling then that I would watch the children, whom I had held in my arms as babies, descend from the sanctity of the round kiva to dance the Corn Dance in the Plaza. They would move up with the years from the end of the line where even the tiny ones shake their gourd rattles and change step with the beat of the drum.

I was brought back to the present by the sound of wagon wheels and the children's voices shouting "Tay-tay, tay-tay," as they ran to meet their grandfather. Soon they came around the corner of the house clinging to Ignacio's hands and apparently telling him how we had waited for him. After greetings and the casual words that always prepare the way for real Pueblo conversation, I explained our errand. There was much talk in Tewa with Susana and Rosalie. Finally Ignacio said, "I think Joe will help you. He can take you to town in his car for the things you need. Then he will go down there to do the work. When he comes in, we'll ask him and see what he says."

Ignacio's idea was just what we had hoped for, and we eagerly waited for Joe to put the horses in the corral. When he came in he grinned as he asked us, "Why don't you catch some of the burros down there so you don't have to walk?" Everyone laughed, knowing full well we couldn't have ridden the wild things even if we had been able to catch them.

Joe was not only handsome but dependable, and when he agreed to his father's proposal, I was satisfied that he would solve the problem. As we walked home, with a warm friendly glow in our hearts, we knew that we were no longer strangers in the valley.

Several weeks later after Joe had cut the south and east sides of the corner room for windows, we were ready to cover the walls. Burlap had been suggested, and when I asked about it at the wholesale mercantile company, Mr. Kelly said, "Why not use wool sacks? They should be long enough for your wall, and we have plenty this year." I came home with rolls of building paper for an inner lining and two dozen wool sacks, feeling akin to the sheepherders who had passed the house recently.

Each year when the snow on the western Jemez Mountains had receded to the highest peaks, these men drove the sheep in their care from winter pastures south of Santa Fe to summer grass in the Valle Grande, an extinct crater become a fertile valley high in the mountains. On a May day an unusual sound would come from across the river and, after a moment of registering and remembering, we would exclaim, "The sheep!" All work would come to a standstill as we ran out into the yard to watch the procession. The four or five burros, heavily laden with bedrolls, food, pans, and small cookstove, crossed the bridge first and waited patiently during the major crisis of the long trek. A cloud of dust and the bleating of many sheep preceded the flock as they came over the foot of the mesa and approached the bridge. The herder who had driven the burros ahead hurried back to stand at the bridge entrance and keep the sheep from going down the steep riverbank. A second herder stood on the opposite side to discourage those who tried to climb the trail. Another ran forward to persuade the leading sheep that a narrow suspension bridge was a safe gateway to water. Sheep must be as perverse as humans. Sometimes they followed their leader across the bridge and down the sloping bank to drink. Sometimes they balked, turned back, or piled up at the entrance, while herders shook tin cans and called in vain, and cars waited impatiently. If slowly melting snows had delayed the journey, the crossing was complicated by lambs on wobbly legs. How the herders finally reassured and cajoled the frightened creatures I never understood, but always the bridge was crossed.

Thirst quenched, the journey was renewed. Sheep and dust followed the river into the canyon, and again the sound was tucked away in memory until frost turned the leaves of the cottonwoods golden, and again brought the sheep to lower levels. The passing of the sheep came to be a seasonal ritual, following that of the changing trees. Both seemed certain, varying only as spring and fall were early or late.

After the sheep had been sheared in the Valle Grande, big wagons piled high with bulging wool sacks crossed the bridge on their way to Santa Fe. By this time, the walls of the house had been covered with sacks of the same kind. They made a soft tan background, restful to eyes tired from the glare of hot summer days, and a pleasant contrast to the brightly colored Navajo rugs on the floor.

When the room was ready for furniture, Joe made tables to fit under the windows and a desk between a pair of bookshelves against the north wall. An iron cot was transformed by a gay cover into a couch, and two chairs seated our guests. When my family learned of the children who came from the Pueblo to visit, they sent from the East a tiny armchair which had been used through many generations. It was the delight of every child who used it, and I came to watch for the lighting of black eyes and the settling of a little body in the old high-backed chair of my childhood. Many pairs of small brown hands had caressed most of the paint off its arms, but the chair was always treated with the utmost care. Years later, on the advent of the first grandchild in the family, it had to be replaced by a Mexican chair, which the children, as well as I, considered a poor substitute.

The Acoma pitcher and bowls came out of their box to be placed on top of the bookshelves with the orange and blue Hopi plaques, the Navajo doll, and the brass candlesticks. Strangely, these last did not seem incongruous. A tiny Indian rabbit carved out of white stone sat among the pictures on the narrow shelf above the desk. On the long table under the south windows, the Cochiti pottery "singing lady" found a place among the books and plants. I never knew what significance she had for the girl who named her; but as she sat out the years with me, she became the symbol of woman's place in the Indian world.

The south windows framed the river and its two mesas, where light and shadow changed with hour and season. Those on the east looked out across the river beyond tall cottonwoods to the Sangre de Cristo Mountains, twenty miles away. There, in gradual ascent, were foothills dotted with juniper, then lower ranges where piñon flourished, higher ranges of pine and aspen, and finally, bare peaks against a brilliant sky. One can never fix these mountains in the mind. Sometimes the light makes each range stand out, casting sharp shadows on the one behind. Occasionally, when the air is very clear, there is a strange and breathtaking, shining light on the green aspen leaves. At evening, the twilight may run quickly from the valley shrouding, almost at once, the highest peaks, or mauve and rose may move slowly upward turning to blood red on the snow above. One morning they may be purple cardboard mountains, sharp-cut against the sky. On another, they will have withdrawn into themselves, their appearance changed completely. One cold gray day, driving to Santa Fe with two Pueblo men who maintained an easy silence, I watched ghost mountains, with substance only in their dark outline. It seemed as if they had gone down into their very roots, leaving an empty frame.

On a morning soon after the living room was finished, a middle-aged Indian with a staff in his hand came walking over the bridge and into the yard. A twisted red bandanna kept the bangs and side-locks of his graying hair from blowing in the June wind. He was not really old, but the years had begun to round his thin shoulders.

Joe looked up from his work to tell us that this was Juan Estevan Roybal, Adam's father-in-law. As I greeted him, he clasped my hand loosely and said, "I look for my cows." This may have been one of the reasons for his walk, but undoubtedly the other was to satisfy his curiosity about the women who lived at the bridge. I suggested that he rest before hunting his cattle and led the way into the living room.

He walked around the room slowly; looked carefully at pictures and books, rugs and pottery. Then he turned to me and said, "Usted muy rico." This was startling, but from my meager Spanish vocabulary I managed to answer, "Oh, no, muy pobre!" He laughed heartily, and, apparently at ease, sat down and lit a cigarette.

The rico-pobre exchange never varied and became the first of much similar repartee during his frequent visits. One day later in the summer he handed me a five-dollar bill. When I looked puzzled, he said, "Always you say you are poor. I bring you some money."

It was difficult to make him understand the difference between poor and destitute, and only when I promised to tell him if I were in need was he satisfied. He had offered me what well may have been the only cash he possessed, for his income was both uncertain and small. In later hours of doubt and insecurity, I remembered his kind eyes and the five-dollar bill.

The kitchen was next on our reconstruction schedule. It never became modern, and its furnishings were most simple. There were only the old stove, left from Shorty's regime, and two chairs which had come from a factory. Joe made doorless cupboards and a table, while Lottie contrived a washstand and a cabinet out of odds and ends of lumber. The water buckets stood on a wooden box in which books had been shipped. Another packing case held cedar wood for the stove. The floor had no covering.

Soon after the china cupboard against the west wall was finished, a trainman called from the mid-weekly freight. "Here's a barrel of dishes come all the way from Pennsylvania. I'll put it off on your side of the track."

We were alone that day, but we managed to roll the barrel over to the house and pry off the top. I was eager to know what the barrel contained, but only when the bottom of the barrel was visible did I stand back and see its contents as a whole. Spread out before me were the dishes I had known in my German grandmother's house when I was a child. They opened a floodgate in my memory.

As I arranged the Meissen plates on the shelves, I thought of my timid little grandmother who as a girl packed her thick Lutheran books in a wooden chest and crossed the Atlantic after her betrothed died.

The little cups with brown figures and the pink lustre plate had no special significance, but the Tucker tea set had belonged to my Welsh grandmother. I had not provided the wedding supper for its traditional use, but since I was establishing a home, the family had decided to send the tea set to me. Into the drab kitchen it brought brightness and color; into the lonely detachment it brought me a sense of continuity.

When I returned to New Mexico and my great longing for a home here was fulfilled, a strong personal feeling for the house developed. But on the day the old china was placed in the cupboard, that feeling began to diminish. It was years later, however, when I fully realized how little the house reflected me, how much even the kitchen represented many influences and many people.

We worked slowly in the west room, which was to be store and tearoom, while we waited for Julian to build a corner fireplace. The walls were covered with wool sacks, and orange paint was ready for door and window frames, but the fireplace was not even started. We were learning how slowly most things move in this land and how futile it is to fret and fume.

To our relief Adam came one day late in June, and, with a note of achievement in his voice, announced, "My uncle Tilano is bringing the adobes for the fireplace in his wagon. Tomorrow he will come to build it."

When I expressed my disappointment that Julian was not going to make the fireplace, Adam's face showed the heaviness of his heart as he replied, "My father is sick again." Gradually I learned that this sickness was not Julian's alone, that it had increased in the Pueblo as a result of the evils of Prohibition when bootlegging permeated the valley and crossed the boundaries of the reservation. Sometimes it hung like a dark cloud over the Pueblo, from which its shadow fell upon the house at the bridge.

After lunch the sound of hoofbeats and the rattle of wagon wheels from across the river verified Adam's words. The driver of the white horses turning into the bridge was Atilano Montoya, governor of the Pueblo and Adam's great-uncle. He was known as "Tilano" to Spanish and Anglos, and was called "Uncle" by many

Indians. This was the first time I had met the short sturdy man who placed his black hat on the floor as he sat down to rest after unloading the adobes.

His face was deeply furrowed, but his hair was still black and the braids hanging in front of his shoulders were thick. He had the dignity and humor common to most Pueblo people, and a warmth and

kindness which gave him many friends. I came to know him as a gentle, patient man who had a real love for people, especially for children. His feeling for people and his desire to make them happy were balanced by a fundamental strength which could be used with severity when necessary. So great was his zest for life that in spite of his years, he would never be old.

I did not know as we talked that Tilano was to be one of the major influences in the development of the house, that without him the years would have been very different.

When he asked me where I came from, and I replied, "Philadelphia," a light came into his eyes and he said, "Philadelphia? I've been there."

"You've been there?" I asked, scarcely believing my ears.

"Yes," Tilano replied, "when I came back from Europe, I stopped in Philadelphia for a little while. Then I came home to the Pueblo."

"You went to Europe?" I exclaimed.

My amazement must have amused him. He smiled and said, "Yes, I went to London, England, to Paris, France, to Rome and to Berlin."

By that time my eyes were like saucers, and I begged him to tell me more.

"Went with Bostock."

"Bostock, the animal trainer?"

"Yes," Tilano said quietly, "he took his animals, their trainers, and five of us from San Ildefonso."

"But how did Bostock happen to know you, and what did you do?" I asked. His story astonished me more and more as it continued.

"Some of us from the Pueblo went to Coney Island one summer to dance. There Bostock saw us and asked if we would go to Europe with him in the fall. Five men decided to go. We were seasick on the boat and were glad to get to England. We stayed in London for a week or two. It was all right, but Paris was the best place and we stayed there a long time—maybe a month or more. The people liked us and clapped lots when we came out on the stage. When we walked on the street, they crowded around us and asked, 'Are you American Indians?' Soon we learned some words of their language and could answer them."

"What did you dance?" I asked.

"The Eagle Dance," Tilano answered, "but not like here in the Pueblo. There we didn't paint our bodies, and we used any kind of feathers to make the eagle wings and tail, but the French liked it."

This was an abbreviated version of the European story, which I heard many times without a change. He never tired of telling tales, whether they were stories told by the "oldest men" or his own experiences. But those things "which must not be told to white people" were not repeated to me or anyone else outside the Pueblo.

Tilano made the transition from Paris in 1908 to Otowi Bridge in 1928 more easily than I did. "I'll bring a helper in the morning," he said as he rose to leave. "It will be hard to make a fireplace in this frame house. I'll have to cut the floor and make a foundation, then a good adobe wall for the back and sides. I guess I'd better bring some clay from near the village, because the dirt here is no good for mud. Show me the place where you want the fireplace, so I can be thinking about it as I drive home. I want to make a good one."

It was a good one. When, at the end of the second day, Tilano started a fire, the draft was perfect. I wanted a low adobe seat built along the wall between the fireplace and the door into the kitchen, but after he had started it, Tilano called me, saying, "It doesn't look right, too long. Go do your work and let me fix it."

When I returned, I found that he had made graduated steps on both sides of the fireplace, the lowest one large enough for a seat. It was much better than my original idea, and I soon saw that the shallow steps could be used to display the black pottery I hoped to sell.

Tilano had set the keynote for the room and given it charm. All I had to do was to keep as unobtrusive as possible, the corner shelves for pottery, the counter for plates of candy and cigarettes, the table and chairs for tea guests. Orange candles in black sconces and gaily colored Chimayo squares brightened the wall and a Navajo rug covered part of the rough floor.

There were windows facing south and west, but I wanted one in the north wall so that while they ate, guests might watch the light change on the Black Mesa. The Spanish-Americans call this mesa Mesita Huérfano because it stands alone beside the river; the Indians call it Tunyo, which means a spot by itself. Probably it was named the Black Mesa long ago by some traveler who came into the valley on a stormy day, and saw for the first time the round dark mass beyond San Ildefonso. It is not always dark and forbidding, for I have seen it when the sun, shining through a rift in the clouds, made it bright and glowing. In formation it is similar to Shumo and To-tavi, the two mesas near the house. Like them it seems drawn upward from the earth with a dark crown of basalt. Unlike these two which stretch for miles on each side of the river, Black Mesa is much smaller and stands out, a solitary unit, against the sky. Undoubtedly individual impressions of the mesa vary, colored by history, legend, or imagination. Before I came to the house by the river, I had associated it with San Ildefonso and my visits there. Now, seen from a greater distance with the Pueblo no longer in the foreground, it stood apart and became for me The Mesa, a "high place" to which my eyes lifted many times a day.

Before the tearoom was entirely ready for business, people began to stop and ask for cold drinks and sandwiches. Ice came out from Santa Fe on the freight train, but between freight-days Coca-Cola bottles were hung in the well, butter and milk were kept in a desert refrigerator, cooled by evaporation. The results must have been passable since some people came again, and slowly the business of the house was established.

Spanish-Americans galloped up to the door and asked for "tobaccy Dukey," crackers and sardines. Covered wagons crossed the bridge and stopped beside the road. From under their canvas covers little children looked out, while an older boy or girl climbed down over the wheel and ran in to ask, "Have you a store? How many candies for a nickel?" Sometimes they wanted cigarettes for the father who held the horses, or a lemon for a coughing child. The whole family would be on its way to their ranchito up on the plateau where they planted pinto beans. All summer long wagons went up and down from beanfields above to chile fields below, and I missed them when the harvest was over and the children went back to school.

All sorts of cars from Model T's to Packards stopped for gasoline at the old pump. The hand crank was so hard to manipulate that I was relieved when the driver wanted only two gallons, in spite of the fact that such small quantities did not pay. If he told me to fill the tank, I learned to suspect that he might say, "I pay you pretty soon, maybe the next time I sell a calf." Sometimes the calf was never sold, and the meager profit for the month was wiped out.

One day when I was especially discouraged, Mr. Gomez and his son came in for sandwiches and coffee. They had come down from their ranch near Los Alamos to celebrate the feast day of St. Santiago. Now they were going home in the mail truck, but it was almost noon and the walk across the valley had made them hungry. When I filled their cups a second time, the old man asked me how much he owed. I knew his family was large and his ranch small, so the amount was half the usual charge. When he paid me, he shook hands and said, "I always like to help a poor lone woman." I thought he referred to the lunch he had bought and was pleased, but when I found the dime he had left under his plate, I decided there were compensations for being "poor and lone."

CHRISTMAS GREETINGS AND REPORTS TO MY FRIENDS

$\mathcal{C}$hristmas was an important time in the Warner household. Edith's niece Sue Smith recalls how most of her family would gather back east during the holidays, and it was a "big thing" to read Edith's yearly Christmas letter aloud and open the box of greens that was her present to them. Sue said Edith and Tilano were "too poor to buy presents." She also remembers how hard it was for her mother, Mary, Edith's youngest sister, to find Tilano's present—yarn the right thickness and shade of turquoise for his hair.[1] Nick King, son of L. D. P. and Edith King, who worked on the Manhattan Project and were regulars at the tearoom, still proudly shows off the childhood Christmas presents Tilano made for him half a century ago: a bow and arrow and a turkey feather headdress in pristine condition.[2] Other kids at the Pueblo and in Los Alamos were given drumsticks with faces painted on the hand-stitched leather heads.[3] Edith got Joan Mark Neary, eldest daughter of Carson and Kathleen Mark, a notebook and put a few recipes in the front, titling it *Joan's Cookbook*.[4] Kay Manley remembers gifts of bundles of piñon kindling tied with red ribbon.[5] Tilano picked dried grass for fireplace brooms.[6] These presents are still keepsakes and heirlooms.

Edith began her Christmas letters in 1942, when the whole country listened to the Murrow news reports on the radio about the boys overseas. These "Christmas Reports" were written, edited, and typed with care. In her letters Edith captured the uniqueness of north-central New Mexico, the birth of the atomic age, and her belief, like Oppenheimer and Bohr, that this new technology should not be left in the control of a few. After Edith finished an original letter, she would mimeograph it, decorate the copies with teacher's star stickers, and put handwritten notes at the end. These letters are now collectors' items, and copies are in several historical and private collections. Edith confessed to her goddaughter after writing the first letter in 1942: "I'm glad the Christmas letter seemed good to you—you undoubtedly get more out of it than anyone. It was something that had to be said, but also had to be pulled out of me. I hadn't courage—or time—to read it before it went out."[7] In Peggy Church's research notes, she wrote that three former teachers said it was Edith's intention to put these letters together one day and publish them.[8] Here they are, with Edith's corrections and a few minor changes.

1943

CHRISTMAS GREETINGS AND A REPORT TO MY FRIENDS
Music—the song of the Rio Grande and the canyon wren
Director—Fate
Narrator—a fearsome woman, whose roots have been shaken but still are deep in the soil of New Mexico

A year ago doubts assailed me. Could I swing this business with gas rationed? Ought I to put aside selfish desire and go back to the outside world and a war job? I had not learned, in spite of much experience, that I am not, and never have been, the guiding hand in my life. Something—what I do not venture to say—has prevented what I thought I wanted to do and pushed me into what I eventually did.

Also, no matter how uncertain the immediate future—or margin-less—a solution has always presented itself in time. But so powerful were those doubts that I had unaccustomed colds and many headaches during the winter. I finally decided to wait and see, having hoarded sufficient for some months. I hope I have learned at long last, for again the unforeseen has happened.

Into this fairly remote section last December came the Army, commandeering Los Alamos School, Anchor Ranch and the small native ranches on all the Pajarito Plateau for some very secret project. The construction company has just completed the building. A new road is almost finished. Many civilians live there and the whole area is guarded by soldiers. Santa Fe calls it a submarine base—as good a guess as any! It leaves only Mrs. Frey at Frijoles and me here at the river—and we are newcomers, comparatively speaking. After about thirty years Los Alamos was dissolved by a stroke of Mr. Stimson's pen—evil magic. Workmen and material began to go by in great quantity so that the valley was quiet no longer. For a year it has continued.

Early in January I was asked on the spur of the moment—yes, a woman is the head—to help in the Indian Service work at San Ildefonso. So I worked on rationing, seed orders, canning, for a small sum until August. It was good to go to the Pueblo and see the people, and I enjoyed it. There are thirteen boys in the armed services and they needed letters. The bill in Congress, threatening the Pueblos, meant more letters.

Tilano and I began planting the garden in warm March days, fearfully—and late in April the unsuspecting fruit blossoms were frozen. However, vegetables survived and produced bountifully and profitably, being sent to Los Alamos all summer. It was good to work in the soil. The garden, where Tilano's father worked, has a special quality as well as its own charm. Even the bears came down to it this fall!

Along about April the X's began coming down from Los Alamos for dinner once a week, and they were followed by others. Stranger even than the Army's choosing this locality was that the civilian head should be a man I knew. He had stopped years ago on a pack trip, come back for chocolate cake, brought a wife, and now was to be my neighbor for the duration. So once again a woman talked women's talk in my kitchen, a child played with Tavi, the dog, and hunted white turkey feathers.

That beginning has increased until there are one or two groups on most nights for dinner. They come in through the kitchen door, talk a bit before leaving, and are booked up weeks ahead. Because they are isolated and need even this change for morale, I feel it is definitely a war job for me. In addition they are mostly interesting and so solve my need for people, though that seems well supplied. There is always someone—the trailer woman coming for milk and eggs, the road camp woman for milk, and both for talk with a woman.

Summer was hot and dry. Dust covered everything; grasshoppers ate Pueblo crops; dump trucks hauled gravel from the riverbed through the yard; surveyors drove stakes all over; drillers brought an infernal machine into the yard to find what foundation the earth offered for a bridge; noise ceased only with nightfall. Fear lived with me—and then suddenly in the fall was lifted. The bridge is not to be built now—lack of material. The road via Española is being repaired. It would have taken part of the yard, perhaps the well house, and the only possible solution for life here seemed a high wall. That would mean that when I stand at the kitchen door, as I so often do for a moment, to look at the mesas, at the cottonwoods' new green or the chamisa golden in the fall, I'd be looking at a wall. Now those moments at the door have deeper meaning.

Peter came in September with a friend. Fortunately there had been no house guests before, for the San Ildefonso women are working at Los Alamos daily and I've had no help. Fall was especially beautiful and I wangled enough free hours to climb mesas and enough gas to go up to Navawi'i (an Indian ruin) for a picnic. All that and the kitchen gabfests compensated for the summer.

Winter means better radio reception, some time to read, walks for mail. I hope there will be snow. I have joined [the] Foreign Policy Association and am reading West and Adamic on Yugoslavia. I still care intensely what happens in the world and wish I required less sleep so I might read more. Tilano has had rheumatism but is better and has discarded his cane. He helps me serve, which satisfies his need and real love of people. Julian's death was hard on him, but he enjoys Juanita's fine boy and Santana's new baby, the children home from school, the soldiers on furlough.

Soon it will be Christmas Eve and Tilano will light the little pitch-wood fire out near the well house to welcome those spirits that draw near on that night. Inside, candles will burn and juniper fragrance will fill the house. Then I shall think of you all and wish that I might share with you the beauty and the peace. The essence of this land fills me at such times—as whenever I give it opportunity—and I know I have been given more than one human's share of joy.

1944

CHRISTMAS GREETINGS AND A SECOND REPORT
TO MY FRIENDS (BY REQUEST)

Music—the song of the Rio Grande and the canyon wren

Director—Fate

Narrator—a reassured woman, who hopes for another year of root-safety

Again I look back across the months to bring you a glimpse of their pattern here by the river. After the confusion and the fears of 1943, this year's peace and beauty stand out like shining peaks. I wish the world might have them, too.

My wish for snow was fulfilled beyond any expectation and the Christmas Eve fire was encircled by fresh white snow. Only the oldest men in the Pueblo remember so much snow on the ground for so many weeks. Temperatures fell to 16 below zero some mornings, bringing thick fog to the valley. There was hoarfrost on every tiny weedstalk and juniper berry and the rising sun shone on it making a magic world for me to go out into for wood and water. I managed to keep the house warm and, with chains, to drive to the Pueblo when necessary. Mostly I walked for mail, breaking the trail after each new snow and enjoying it. It was wonderful to look out at my mesas and see them all white—especially after the very dry preceding winter. It meant grass for cattle, water in the ace-quias for fields, a continued life cycle for seeds waiting underground through dry years. Bad roads were something to be endured and forgotten.

The Los Alamosers, who had skiing until May, came all through the winter five nights a week for dinner until my arm rebelled and then my gall bladder. So after several weeks' rest, I reduced the weekly average to three nights, which I have maintained. With the increased population "on the hill" I could serve every night and still have a waiting list. My contact with them is necessarily casual but interesting and there are some I should like to know better. How long they will be there is as secret as what they are doing. Building seems to continue, though I am scarcely conscious of it now that the Española road has been oiled. Only a few workmen and civilians come this way, to my great relief.

Spring was late in coming but when it did the snow-fed ground burst forth with flowers I had never seen. The juncos, bluebirds, towhees that fed at the window tray all winter stayed on and many others came. Peas were planted on a cold windy day and the peach blossoms never opened, but there were violets late in March—the first I have persuaded to grow. I fixed a perennial bed near the acequia with plants from Allene's garden and put a table near it under an old apple tree. There Tilano and I ate our lunch on planting days.

On one of those days I crossed the arroyo hoping to find new flowers. Above it on a stony little hill I came suddenly on three Mariposa lilies, the first I had ever seen down here. In the Valle Grande high in the Jemez there are many lavender Mariposas, but here in the valley they are white with golden centers—exquisitely beautiful. There was no contentment then until I had climbed what Hewitt calls Mariposa Mesa "where thousands bloom." The old trail was almost gone but Tilano found a way to the top where I again found three lilies. The seeds must have waited patiently through all these dry years for enough moisture to germinate them.

There on that ruinless mesa we found a stone ax and a broken pottery bowl, left by some ancient farmer. Why? When? What did he think and feel? These are the things I ponder as I gather shards— edges, handles, designs all varying as did their makers. I have missed those "ruining" trips during the war, but this year we combined wood-getting and picnics and so got up on the mesas numerous times. This spot on the river is home and I always return to it eagerly, but it is good to go up to the levels above and look out across the world and back into the past. That is especially true now with the Pueblo boys in France, England and the Pacific. Slim was wounded soon after D-Day in Normandy but has recovered for more duty. Brownie's ship soon sails. Hilario's destroyer has seen action. Rafael hasn't seen his son for over a year. Sandy feels walled in by the jungle. Two have had two years in Alaska and go out to another theatre. I look into the future of their return and adjustment with concern.

In spite of the late spring and strange summer weather, the garden did well. Two of the little boys came to help Tilano and twice a week we sent vegetables up to Los Alamos. The surplus, after house and dinner guests were fed, went into jars and the rootcellar shelves are filled. It was former houseguests who came, understanding the lack of help and willing to have no service. So again there was talk of many things and contact with the outside that I need and enjoy.

The last guest was Peter who came in the fall. Again I climbed mesas joyfully on non-L.A. days and looked at golden trees, forgetting the house. The woodpile grew and the garden harvest was brought in. Wild geese flew south on many days—circling, honking, reforming the silver V above the house to continue on their certain way. The flight of the geese, the deer tracks on the mesas, the first green and the final golden leaves of the cottonwoods, Venus low above the mesa—all these recur.

After Christmas I am going to rest for a month or two, hoping to regain some lost weight. There is a pile of Survey Graphics, Inter-Americans, Foreign Policy bulletins, in addition to a package of books, for reading. There will be walks for mail and to the Pueblo to see the new babies. With new batteries there should be music and news. Some evenings Tilano will tell tales of long ago. Seed catalogues will come in and another garden be planned. I look forward to it all.

As the flames of the Christmas Eve fire leap into the night, I shall think of my friends with gratitude and with joy.

1945

THE THIRD CHRISTMAS REPORT TO MY FRIENDS

New Year's day of this historic 1945 held no hint of the atomic era. There were no blasts from the Pajarito Plateau making discord in the song of the chorus as I sat in the sun on an old portal at San Ildefonso. Teen, just past two, watched the dancers with me and later demonstrated the steps of the little deer. The only indication of war was the absence of his father and the other young men.

During January I rested and learned to milk, but the Pueblo prepared for San Ildefonso's feast day on the 23rd. It was the time for the ceremonial Buffalo dance and once again I took Tilano over to the house where he and all the dancers would make themselves ready. On the morning of the fourth day they went into the hills before dawn to await the haunting song of the chorus. I leaned against an old adobe house as the deep drum tones rolled and the song called the men who danced as godly animals. For hundreds of years a chorus has called and a line of women waited at the foot of the hill— waited to touch these men and take into themselves that intangible spiritual power sometimes attained by human beings. As the song reached its climax, a long gray plumed serpent of smoke rose from the hilltop and spread over the pueblo. From between the hills came the leader, the hunters, the Buffalo lady and men. From over the hills came Deer and Antelope and Mountain Sheep. All came to the foot of the hill where the women waited to touch them, where the chorus waited to accompany them to the plaza with an exultant song.

Tilano, who has always been a Deer, became the leader this year. Babies I had held were grown enough to be Antelope and Sheep. Tomacita and Facundo were Buffalo and their son slept in his cradle in the ceremonial house while they danced. These human bonds made contact for me, so that the snow falling softly and quietly on the earth, on deer antlers and buffalo manes and curved sheep horns, was significant.

Pruning was finished but the first peas had not been planted when Joe came to tell me that his father, Ignacio, had gone on his last journey to the hills. It was to Ignacio's house that John Boyd had taken me 23 years ago. It was Ignacio who had told me, "If, when we dance, our hearts are right, the rain will come." There were many memories as I watched the candles flicker at his side—memories of him and those others who had preceded him. Just the month before, stooped and almost blind, he had served at the mass for Tonita. He had lived a long, full, active life. The moccasins beneath his blanket were well worn. He would have been unhappy sitting by the fire. I miss him as I still miss Juan Estevan and Sayah, but I cannot mourn.

Summer was dry and hot—so hot. I searched in vain for Mariposa lilies in June though the hills had been gay with flowers in May. The weeks seemed an endless round of gathering vegetables and preparing meals. There was tension and accelerated activity on the Hill (Los Alamos) with the men "going south" (to the Alamogordo site). Explosions on the Plateau seemed to increase and then to cease. Men were in the Pacific, leaving wives on the Hill. Things—unknown things—were happening.

The climax came on that August day when the report of the atomic bomb flashed around the world. It seemed fitting that it was Kitty Oppenheimer who, coming for vegetables, brought the news. She was the woman in my kitchen of the first report and wife of the Director. I had not known what was being done up there, though in the beginning I had suspected atomic research. Much was now explained. Now I can tell you that Conant and Compton came in through the kitchen door to eat ragout and chocolate cake; that Fermi, Allison, Teller, Parsons came many times; that Oppenheimer was the man I knew in pre-war years and who made it possible for the Hill people to come down; that Hungarians, Swiss, Germans, Italians, Austrians, French and English have been serious and gay around the candlelit table. It has been an incredible experience for a woman who chose to live in a supposedly isolated spot. In no other place could I have had the privilege of knowing Niels Bohr, who is not only a great scientist but a great man. In no other way could I have seen develop a group feeling of responsibility for presenting the facts to the people and urging the only wise course—international control of atomic energy and bombs.

Perhaps the desperate state of the world and the anguish of millions as the constant backdrop of life intensified the joys that fall always brings. This year there were trips to the Plateau for wood on days when sky and aspens vied with each other in beauty. The wind made melody in tall pines while I gathered pine knots, those multi-shaped legacies of long forgotten trees. They seem to be the essence of the elements garnered by a tree and now released in the fireplace to complete the cycle. Their gathering has become as much a part of the fall ceremonies as the garden harvesting and the southward flight of the wild geese. This rhythmic order of nature holds for me assurance as well as beauty.

Perhaps a similar human need is satisfied when people return to this spot and find it unchanged. Los Alamos boys bring wives and babies and hope there is a piece of remembered cake, which has become a symbol. The new Los Alamos people leave, planning to come back. But this is a changing world. Perhaps what they really want is to find the essence unchanged. That becomes my challenge.

And now it is December, with longed-for snow clouds advancing and retreating. Today Tilano and I went for Christmas greens. With ample gas we could go in search of fir and we chose Water Canyon where the old Frijoles road climbed up on the mesa in my tenderfoot days. Today there were fresh deer and turkey tracks in the road and pieces of fir under a tree brushed by antlers. Snow flurries hid Los Alamos but sun shone on Tsacoma, the sacred mountain of the west.

On this Christmas Eve some of the Pueblo boys will help to light the little fires. Others will be homeward bound. The war is over. Peace is still to be secured. The scientists know that they cannot go back to their laboratories leaving atomic energy in the hands of the armed forces or the statesmen. Nor can I concern myself only with my kitchen, for I, too, am one of the people.

As the pitch wood of the fire releases its stored energy here by the river when Christmas Eve darkens the mesas my thoughts and wishes will go out in all directions to you, my friends.

1946

THE FOURTH CHRISTMAS REPORT TO MY FRIENDS

This year really began on the Sunday before Christmas 1945. That day I was taken up to Los Alamos for the first time since the school commencement in June 1941. Falling snow softened outlines of trailer camps, hutments, apartments, barracks, machine shops. Barbed wire secured but did not hide the "Tech Area," where men had worked tensely a few months before to bring into being the atomic bomb. Here a new era had begun, but the normal reaction of excitement was overshadowed by the terrifying possibilities of this new power.

The Pueblo had long looked forward to Christmas, when the boys would be home. Some did come and Rafael realized his dream of two Christmas Eves in England to be Santa Claus at the school party. Tall, diffident, wounded Slim, whom the children adore, was home at long last and came over here with them for the annual party. I shall never forget that group, from sixth-graders to toddlers, sitting on the floor around the Christmas tree and looking up at Slim as they sang his request—"Silent Night."

By the time Peter came in February it was evident that problems had been intensified, not solved by war—communal as well as international. Always we hope for a magic word or touch, but human relationships have to be worked at. Feeling the urgency, we put our minds to work, but minds alone are not sufficient. So we went out into the sunshine and walked beside the river where slender grasses made swaying shadows and tiny animals left miniature tracks on the sand. We looked long at the pattern of a mesa made by the centuries and knew that waiting and believing were essential, too.

In the Pueblos old ceremonial dances were being revived. Some I had never seen, others not for years. It was good to see a long line of men and boys dancing with the women bringing baskets of cornmeal and bread to place before them. It was with awe that I watched a sinking Easter sun shine on men's dancing bodies painted yellow and on the spreading eagle feathers of the women's headdress. Soldiers and sailors had returned from Europe and Japan to lay aside uniforms and wear again ceremonial kirtles and moccasins. Could the habits of war be so easily discarded?

Spring came early after a dry winter. Wild geese flew north in February and leaves were unfolding as I pruned the raspberries. Some peach and apricot blossoms defied the calendar and paid the penalty. But no rain came with the spring. The sun blazed and dry winds blew. Plants in the garden struggled to live. Wildflowers that braved the drought soon faded. Grass turned brown and crackled underfoot. The Valle Grande, that beautiful green crater high in the Jemez, was brown in June with sheep and cattle only in the narrow strip of green beside the stream. Water was rationed in Santa Fe. Some of us recalled another year of drought when cattle lay dead on the hills—and were fearful. Tree rings had vivid meaning.

Then early in July there was a miracle. Rain came and after only a few short storms the grass was green. Trees held up their leaves. Plants began to grow. Human nerves relaxed. Fears receded as we forgot how helpless we are without rain. When I saw the Valle Grande in September, it was luxuriantly green and cattle were fat. Fringed gentians grew beside a stream. The broom grass mesa was a tapestry of red paintbrush, many blue and yellow asters, graceful grasses and pine tree shadows.

Summer brought houseguests, the vegetable business and canning—necessitating an interlude in the Los Alamos dinners. It brought, too, congenial evenings in the starlight and early mornings in the garden picking raspberries while hummingbirds whirred and whirled.

After the September Corn Dance, opening chamisa buds took up the golden challenge of fall, begun by the smaller wildflowers. Cottonwoods followed until the valley shone. On the lagoon a pair of white egrets and the blue herons stood motionless, reflected with the sky in the water. The kingfisher drove away an intruder on his domain. Grosbeaks moved in to noisily eat the bumper crop of juniper berries. It was time to prepare for winter and we went happily up on the Plateau to gather pineknots for the fireplaces. Now, as I recall the feel of warm sunshine, the smell of pine needles, the sound of the wind high in the trees, the peace of the little canyon, I find myself contrasting that fuel-getting with the mining of coal.

Such mental questioning and awareness of the world prompted formation of a small discussion group here in the valley. It is an attempt to increase our share of public opinion by pooling our information and clarifying our reactions. Most of us find it an incentive and a mental stimulus. Perhaps, too, it is a beginning of community awareness. We, all Anglos, are the newcomers in a valley long inhabited by Spanish-Americans and Indians—a small scale world. My hope is a real community group.

As a balancing factor there is always the fascinating past of the Pajarito Plateau and its people, to whose personality bits of broken pottery and artifacts offer a clue—which seems to have given me a hobby. This fall as I rested on the ruined wall of Navawi'i I heard a familiar sound. Looking up, my vision finally caught a thin silver V far above the ruin—wild geese southward bound. I had always thought of geese as following the river. Now I knew that some used the Plateau for their high road and that Navawi'i women must have listened, too, and watched that undulating silver line against the blue fall sky, then hastened their preparation for winter.

Today we gathered the Christmas greens. Large Los Alamos signs bar the canyons where we formerly found fir—even Water Canyon where last year a wild turkey's feather lay beside his tracks. Most of the men whose knowledge made atomic bombs possible have returned to laboratories and universities to do research, to teach future scientists, to try to solve the world atomic problem. But others have come to continue work on atomic weapons as well as other uses of the energy. So louder and louder blasts echo over the Plateau and my blood runs cold remembering Hiroshima. If the world lived here, all would be reminded frequently that we must catch up with striding science and find a way to live together in the peace that Christmas signifies.

The little wood is ready for the Christmas Eve luminario. As I watch its bright flames and listen to the song of the river, my Christmas wishes will go out across the mesas to you.

1947

THE FIFTH CHRISTMAS REPORT TO MY FRIENDS
When Tilano lights the little pitch fire on Christmas Eve, those to whom it pays respect will know that human beings now live where last winter only quail, rabbits and coyote made patterns in the snow. The wild geese discovered it when they flew south—some coming very low over the new house. But the blue heron has not followed us from the river to the side of To-tavi-kadi—mesa of the quail. I miss hearing him as he flew homeward after his late supper; miss seeing him standing on one leg in the lagoon as he waited for a minnow to swim across his image on the water. I miss the song of the river, though once I heard it here on a still night. Most of all I miss the rhythmic line of To-tavi against the sky with sunset clouds, a new moon or the evening star above it.

For many the little house at the river was a landmark, for some an experience. For me it was two decades of living and learning. I had hoped to live out my life "where the river makes a noise." The house is still there and surely its walls retain the personality developed through the years from those who came into it, left a little of themselves and went away remembering its simplicity and peace. Each has his own special memory, be it chocolate cake, the scrubbed boards of the kitchen floor or the Black Mesa framed by a window. For me, at this period, two are especially vivid. I still stand in the kitchen doorway looking into the canyon of the singing river and up at the two great mesas glistening with snow, dark with rain, everchanging but always steadfast. The other is going into the adobe dining room—darkened against the sun and cool after the kitchen's heat. It was very still and serene and yet alive with the strength of those for whom it had meaning.

When last year's letter went out, I knew that a new bridge would bring the road through the yard very close to the house and that the Los Alamos traffic would be unendurable. Tilano refused to leave, but when I found an open space across the arroyo from the garden, he reconsidered. So when Marie and Adam's family came for supper on Christmas Eve and the children helped light the pitch fire, I knew that it was the last Christmas by the river.

Sitting here beside the fireplace in Tilano's sunny room with its beautiful view of the mountains, it seems as though a miracle had been performed this year. The months of waiting for a decision about these four acres of Pueblo hillside and the difficulties of building are overshadowed by a truly remarkable manifestation of friendliness. The result is a comfortable house above the arroyo, southeast of the garden and just beneath the basaltic columns where the mesa forms a point. It looks out over the cottonwoods of Tony's fields to the mountains and up the wide arroyo to carved gray mesa points. The mesa to the north towers over it, shutting out the Black Mesa but giving its own rugged outline. To-tavi shelters it from the southwest wind and reflects the winter sun. Eventually trees will protect from that same reflection in summer. Juniper and a few piñon trees, New Mexican olive and spice bushes, chamisa and cactus give it a natural garden and spring should bring wildflowers. It is still a very new house but time will blend it with the earth from which it came and give it charm, I hope.

Looking back to those dry windy spring days when I was faced with building a house and a road, finding water, moving stable, corral and chickenhouses, I am certain it was a miracle. I had only a few hundred dollars and some old lumber. But Tilano and I had friends—more than we knew. There were those who had found in the guest-house rest for weary bodies and minds; those who had watched the morning light move across the mesas and been renewed. They made possible the beginning and early in May, Tony Pena came from the Pueblo to make adobe bricks in the garden, where corn grew the year before.

Rain fell on those first adobes but did not damage them. The foundation was laid out in the rain. Tony and Tilano looked happy and said it was good. Now there is snow and Tilano smiles knowingly. There will be grass for the cattle in the spring, water for the fields and perhaps Mariposa lilies. It is probable that the arroyo will have water in it all spring, but we can cross it on horseback or in the wagon. No difficulty seems too great when the land has water.

Last May, too, we came in wagons for there was no road. It was the day of the foundation laying. Facundo and Sandy, Tony and Juanita brought their wagons, and a group from Los Alamos, who had asked to help, worked with them. Men hauled rocks, women fitted them into the trench and mixed mud. Children played in the arroyo water hole and rode in the wagons. It was a good day and I use good as Tilano does when he speaks of rain.

That was just the beginning of many such days—days of hard work in the heat broken by lunch in the meadow. There under the big cottonwoods as they relaxed after lunch, physicists conferred with Tony and Tilano on adobe construction problems. Walls rose and the roof went on—a roof made of old vigas from the Pueblo, new ones from Truchas and Puye, and across them peeled pine saplings covered with roofing paper, mud, more paper and tar, more dirt—a good roof.

When it was time to cover the walls with plaster—first rough, then smooth—the Pueblo people sent word that they wanted to do it. The men mixed the mud and carried it inside to the women. Some kneaded it and handed it to those who, with skilled hands, covered the adobe bricks. There was much talk and laughter and always a beautiful rainbow motion of the hand, so that I look now at the walls and see those plastering days as a rainbow. Old beams were brought for the portal; lumber was found for frames; horses and tools were loaned. More than once I was told, "You don't have to pay me. I want to help."

There were also those who gave their interest, advice and belief, like mortar holding bricks together. Most of you knew nothing of this project, but you had faith in what the old house stood for. It was all of this that gave me courage to clear the many hurdles, as well as appreciation of the fundamental kindness of man.

From this house made from the earth by many hands and hearts, there will go on Christmas Eve to the Pueblo, the Valley, the Hill, on and on across the mesas and mountains, appreciation as warm as the flames from the little fire and the wish that the new house may share its joy with you.

1948

SIXTH CHRISTMAS LETTER

The December moon, a silver crescent above the hill to the south, sends my thoughts back a year to the first Christmas in this house. The little pitch fire blazing up into the twilight of Christmas Eve must have startled the wild creatures whose tracks marked the snow. Tilano and I watched until only embers remained, thinking gratefully of those who had made possible the new house and of all who wished it well.

After the Matachines dance in the Pueblo on Christmas day, Adam brought his family, Maria and Clara, Desideria and Donicio for dinner. The new kitchen was gay with a tiny decorated tree, red candles on the wall and the long table, as eager-eyed children and laughing grown-ups watched me carve the turkey. If walls take into themselves the scenes they witness, a recording of a happy Christmas must be there in the kitchen's hand-smoothed adobe. As our guests were leaving, the northern mesa stood out so clearly in the moonlight that I was moved to tell Donicio about the eagle I recently had seen circling above the mesa before flying south over To-tavi.

The cough Donicio had that night developed into pneumonia and before New Year's day he had been buried in the churchyard. He was the center dancer in a line dance; the chorus grouped itself around him for the Corn Dance; the song seemed to come from him. Now the center was gone—gone like the eagle I again saw flying south on the day he died. Low clouds hung over the Pueblo as we followed his body to the church; at twilight snow fell softly; in the morning the sun shone on a thick white blanket. A deep feeling of loss followed mourning, and remained. There were no winter or spring dances except, on San Ildefonso day, the Comanche dance, which is not ceremonial.

In January a succession of storms piled snow upon snow. A hand snow-plow cleared necessary paths and the road. The temperature hovered around fifteen degrees below zero many nights. The wood-pile, neglected during the moving, dwindled fast and we had to bring cottonwood logs from the meadow on the sled. However, we managed to be warm, at least near the fireplace, and to keep well. The road was impassable many days, but fortunately the stable and the larder were well-stocked. I worried about Tilano's shoveling so much snow and helped all I could, especially on the roof, which had to be done before the walls became wet. Snow and wood kept us busy.

Tilano's room became a winter sitting-room since all day it has sunlight, a wood-conserver. On stormy days I read to him while he tied parrot feathers for the dancers. The radio brought music, news and his favorite programs. On windless days the sun made the sheltered corner beside the kitchen door warm enough for an outdoor tray-lunch, while the dogs played in the snow nearby. Each trip to the woodpile or the chicken yard was into a world where white mesas glistened against a deep blue sky, where snow-covered trees shook starry flakes from their branches. From the wide window near the fireplace we saw storm clouds gather over the mountains or sunset turn the peaks blood-red. It was a hard winter, but a good one.

As I watched the geese fly north late in February, I thought apprehensively of all the snow that must reach the river via the arroyo which our road crosses. However, an early thaw, which melted the snow here in the valley, was followed by cold weather so that the runoff from higher levels was gradual. We waded several summer flash-floods and rebuilt a short stretch of road, but the arroyo proved itself not the bogy I had feared.

All through the weeks of snow and mud, I thought of spring flowers and hoped I would find a Mariposa lily. Before the last ragged snow-patches on the hillside had melted, the sheltered spots were gay with blossoms—pink, lavender and yellow. One day I noticed a slender stalk near the well and watched it hopefully. After a similar winter I had found three Mariposa lilies above the arroyo and three more high on a mesa. Since then I had looked in vain. Now I waited eagerly for a bud to open and assure me that I had not dreamed an exquisite cream-colored lily with center of gold. At last the solitary stalk and five more below the house bore blooms, were treasured and remembered as a gift of the snow.

June brought heat, and the Corn Dance in the Pueblo. The people prepared anxiously; for they knew that the chorus had lost its former center and strength. But the day was windless; the dance was good; and they felt, as I did, that Donicio was there helping both dancers and chorus.

Guests came with summer and the living-room couch and a cot on the back porch served as beds. The living room, darkened against the sun, became the cool place where I went for rest and renewal as I had to the adobe dining room of the old house. The portal with its view of the mountains was comfortable by mid-afternoon and there we usually ate supper. Happily we showed many visitors the new house and from the reaction of those who knew the old one, I began to feel that the transplanting had been successful, that in time peace might be felt here, too.

The bridge, its superstructure covered with aluminum paint, was finished by midsummer. The old houses show the wear and tear of many children with a family in each. Tavi was hit by a truck and no more begs for a stone to chase.

In August Adam's family came for a traditional dinner. The tall slender sailor, who looked at me before he blew out the candles on his nineteenth birthday cake, was Co-ha. Several months earlier he had worn a cap and gown, but always I see him as a baby being christened, a chubby two-year-old calling me "Co-o Warner," a sturdy eight-year-old helping Tilano in the garden.

We were glad to have several families from Los Alamos plant part of the garden this year. It provided escape from the Hill for the men, fun for the children, and renewal for the women, who recognized the special quality of the garden. Lois, who came down frequently to pick vegetables, took the excess up to the Hill and sold it to her friends for us. After the harvest, the men helped Tilano prepare the garden for winter, continuing group work.

With the help of some of the women, I "made a feast" for the

Pueblo in September. About a hundred came in cars and wagons to see the new house and have dinner. I am glad we did it, but I think a family at a time is more satisfactory. Tomacita and Facundo celebrated their tenth wedding anniversary here. Nahn-tu, their son, who has great charm, now shares attention with a beautiful baby sister and Teen, his cousin, goes to school this year.

Fall was especially wonderful with many trips for wood when I again heard the wind in the pines and gathered pineknots for warmth and the good of my soul. Near a ruin we found a trail worn deep in the rock and a woman's thumbprint still visible on a sherd of her pottery. Once while the men chopped wood beside the new wide road on the Plateau, I walked along a mesa until I no longer heard the traffic. There alone in the sunlight I began to understand that nothing man may do, not even the atomic bomb, can in any way touch or change the essence of this country.

Perhaps when Tilano lights the little pitch fire on this Christmas Eve the deer, whose tracks he saw at the foot of the hill, will pause and watch the flames carry up into the night and across the continent our Christmas wish for peace and beauty.

1949

CHRISTMAS 1949

Gaily wrapped jars of jam, ready for the Christmas Eve trip to the Pueblo, remind me that despite mountains marked with only faint lines of snow and cottonwoods still covered with dry bronze leaves, it is the season for translation of this year's living into words.

Last Christmas Eve as I waited in the dusk for the outdoor rehearsal of the Matachines dance two little boys climbed into the truck with me and in high clear voices sang carols until the fires in front of each house were lighted. Later when Tilano and I left the Pueblo, embers glowed around the plazas and the cold air was pungent with smoke. As we passed the old house, we signaled the children there and by the time we reached home, their two little fires were blazing in the darkness. Tilano quickly lit the two he had laid and as we watched the flames against the dark mesa, we seemed part of a great circle—a Christmas circle of candles in windows, little fires in the night, hearts gladdened by sharing.

Two years of sun and snow have weathered the new house and rooted it deeply on the side of the sheltering mesa. Some of the problems created by the change have been solved. The yield of garden, cow, chickens, kitchen in the form of bread and jam, supplemented by two annual houseguests, has provided a living. This would be impossible without the friends who devote time and energy to delivery. Also it depends somewhat upon the vagaries of the weather, the insect world, and the creatures themselves. However, any meagerness of return is offset by the lack of strain and the increased leisure to enjoy our surroundings and people. Fortunately our needs are simple and are well supplied with a woodpile, alfalfa for Topsy and a larder stocked against storms.

It is true that my primary concern two years ago was a place where Tilano could live out his span happily, since without him the twenty years at the bridge would have been impossible. So his room was planned first and as he wanted it. But the house—this house built by many—could not be justified for us alone. It was essential that it have meaning for others. How was it possible to develop quickly that which at the old house had grown slowly and unplanned over a long period of years? How could it be shared when no commercial reason drew people? For these problems there were no established methods. It was not a picture to be painted, a poem to be written. It was not even mine to create. So I lived each day as it presented itself and hoped I would find the way. During my thinking of this summary for you, it has become clear. Perhaps I can make you see how the growing spirit of this house is compounded of the earth itself and the seasons, of daily living and in great measure of the people who come to it. For they have come.

When I go to feed the chickens each morning, my eyes make the circle of the compass, beginning with the basaltic point of Totavi in the west. Memory supplies its long line above the river, the quiet place on its side where I go to be alone, a tiny crescent ruin covered with dry grasses that shone in the sun, and across the river the carved face of Shumo, whose northern point is visible. Beyond the valley rise the mountains with Lake Peak sharply outlined against the sky and in the north T'omo, like a great outstretched prehistoric creature above the road to Los Alamos. These deeply rooted, steadfast mesas provide a bulwark for living in this age, and at the same time present beauty everchanging in color and aspect. On their sides and high places are ceremonial trails and shrines where for centuries men have placed prayer plumes when their hearts were right. Closer and more intimate is the hillside with its old trail, where I have found stones carried long ago in a buckskin pouch. From it the quail come down near the house and a rabbit who nibbles grass unafraid. Above it the crescent winter moon shines and this month Venus as the evening star.

I am glad that the first winter was one of storm and cold because it necessitated spending many more hours indoors. Tilano's room with its fireplace, and sunlight on clear days, quickly became the lived-in center of the house. Here hang his dance costume—buckskin leggings, foxskin, bells—and pictures of the children who call him uncle. Here feathers are sorted and tied with care for the dancers; a headdress or bow and arrows are made for some child; and from his chair he watches in unceasing wonder the cars going to and from Los Alamos. Sometimes there are guests for tea as color follows color from foothills to sky. Sometimes on winter evenings there are tales of long ago. From here he went, when it was time to prepare for the Buffalo dance, to the Pueblo, and returned with the quality of those days spent apart still about him.

The life cycle reaches the house, too, with Brownie inviting us to his wedding, Sandy unable to hide his happiness at the birth of a son. And inevitably there is word of death—of little Oma-peen, of Susana, my friend of many years, of John Boyd, who first took me to San Ildefonso. It was he who told me Indian lore, taught me to watch for tracks on the trail, showed me the significance a stone might have. He never saw this house but his influence is here.

One evening as I washed dishes, the sound of a long story in Tewa reached me from Tilano's room. When I went in later, Sandy was sitting where he could hear every word and see every expression, and Tilano, looking up with his face aglow, explained, "I am telling Sandy about the Shalako." This year his great desire to see the Shalako at Zuni has been fulfilled and he relives the experience with each eager listener.

I wish you might see the big kitchen on some Sundays, on Thanksgiving, during Christmas week, on many a day throughout the year. Sometimes it is little blonde children, sometimes black-haired children who run into the kitchen for a drink of water or the basket of toys, go with Tilano to gather the eggs or milk the cow. A car may come from Santa Fe, the Hill or across the valley with someone who needs to sit awhile here and look at the mountains or the hillside. Rosanita came to celebrate her graduation as a nurse, Louis and Juanita their wedding anniversary. Hagi, who used to help in the garden as a little boy and who hauled all the water for the house-building, came with his parents after graduation to discuss his future. Several months later he returned in a Marine uniform to tell us "all about it" and how often he thought of his uncle. Peter and Earle bring weeks of merriment and talk. All year our friends and friends of theirs drive across the arroyo to see how we fare, to look at the mountains, to add a bit of themselves to the spirit of the house.

Rain and snow have come to the dry earth since I began to write and there may be a white hillside as a background for the Christmas Eve fire. We shall watch it and the star above it while we wish you joy—joy in many little things through all the year.

1950

CHRISTMAS 1950
Tilano is making a feather headdress, bows and arrows, tiny doll moccasins with silver buttons, for the boys and girls to whom he is a special friend. We have gathered the pitch wood for the little fires; and soon you will be expecting this record of the year from the house on the side of the mesa.

As I sit beside the fireplace and think back across the months,

I realize that during the whole year my eyes have been scanning the sky for clouds, as now. On San Ildefonso day, January 23, I napped on the ground in a sunny spot. In February we disheartedly put away the snow plow. On Easter the wind blew stinging sand in the faces of the Buffalo dancers all day long. Trees blossomed early and the newly formed fruit trees froze in May. Twentieth Century Fox filmed Two Flags West at San Ildefonso and cursed the windblown dust. Water in the irrigation ditch ran slowly day and night while the early corn and beans dried up in the June heat. Early in July the spell seemed broken by a pouring rain that gladdened our hearts and found every hole in powder-dry flat roofs; but in no time the earth was dry again. The Navajos had the clouds seeded for rain while they hauled water for their sheep; and one of their old medicine men journeyed to the four sacred mountains to perform a ceremony for rain. Clouds darkened the western sky and showers fell on the Plateau, sometimes fell with such force that the arroyo, dry all spring, became a rushing torrent. Here in the valley the sun shone as we watched the water wash out the road and fill the garden ditch with gravel. What was left of the garden and our jumpy nerves was saved by the lower temperatures of this strange summer in which the tomatoes were better than ever before. Late one September day Tilano glanced at a dark cloud appearing over the mesa and decided to milk early. Before he had finished, the cloud shed all its hail and rain, which poured off the mesa like waterfalls to make new arroyos and deepen old ones, and washed the mud plaster off the house and under the doors and windows. Since then we can count the drops that have fallen. Carrots were dug with a pick and we have not tried to plow. Day after day we sit in the sun while every bit of moisture evaporates.

I keep thinking of those prehistoric people who left the Plateau during a long drought, left the pueblos where we find potsherds and arrow points in the rubble. They, too, must have scanned the sky with hope and finally with despair before they decided to leave their homes and sacred places, to journey to the south. As the Pueblo tale of their ancestors goes, the lazy ones stayed beside the river and made a new home here in the valley. Were they really lazy or did they have faith that their ceremonies still had power to bring the rains again? Always, even in the driest times, Tilano shakes his head emphatically and says, "He has to come."

Tilano, who is about eighty, seems younger this year and very well. With such a small garden, the summer was not strenuous, save for fixing the road each time the arroyo ran, and there have been no special worries until the recent Korean news. If he can work slowly in his own routine and be free from worry, he still can accomplish a great deal. In the evening he relaxes in his easy chair while he listens to the radio or a favorite book. Almost every day brings someone from far or near to see us, so that he is not lonely. For this I am especially glad since I have not been very well and thus not too companionable. However, rest and diet are bound to bring me back to normal and mesa-climbing soon.

Co-ha and Hagi, the boys who worked with Tilano in the garden from the time they could pull a weed, came home on leave before going overseas. We had the traditional family dinners with a chocolate cake for the boy to cut, but this time the gaiety was only on the surface. Five of the boys from the Pueblo have gone and again, after so short a span, the postman is awaited anxiously. But always the cycle moves on and now the youngest boy in that family comes with his cousin to spend the day, to follow Tilano around and to love him.

Several days have passed—days of clouds and of snow above our level. Now the sky is clearing and the clouds in the east have dropped just below the Truchas peaks, which glisten in the sun. I am sure that I know how the hearts of those long-ago people lightened and with what gratitude they thanked their gods.

How to endure the manmade devastating period in which we live and which seems almost as hopeless to control as drought; how to proceed when leadership seems utterly lacking, when individuals and nations seem stupid and arrogant; these no one human can answer. I only know that the power recognized by those other sky-scanners still exists, that contact is possible. I know, too, what depths of kindness and selflessness exist in my fellow man. Of this I have had renewed assurance recently, when those about me have shared self and substance.

When Tilano lights the Christmas Eve fire, perhaps against a white hillside, I shall watch from the house where some have felt peace and hope that in your sky there are some bright stars.

ESSAYS

Published Essays

During her lifetime, Edith published several pieces in magazines, journals, and literary collections. I did only minimal editing on these pieces, such as deleting archaic hyphens and changing archaic spellings. Edith probably would have published much more if she hadn't spent most of her time working in the tearoom. What little time she had for writing she used to keep up with correspondence and her journal.

I didn't include a few short pieces published in *Space* because they are quotes from Edith's journal. I also left out "The Blazed Trail" (August 1925), "A Closed Door" (December 1925), "Getting Back" (November 1926), and "Narrow Gauge Meals" (May 1926), from the *Philosophy of Health* journal. They were written for hire to attract patients to the Tilden facility in Denver where Edith worked and have little other interest. For the rest of her life Edith did follow the practices of healthy eating and stress relief that she learned at Tilden, and the meals she later served at her tearoom were influenced by her time in Colorado.

In Edith Warner's writing about the San Ildefonso pueblo, she shows her respect for and understanding of these people who became her greatest friends. Edith "never learned to speak Tewa," her goddaughter Peter remembered, "because she wanted the village people to have the privacy of their own language." Peter also remarked how "some of her closest friendships were almost wordless—communication was of another kind. Juan Estevan had almost no English . . . [but] she understood him. Sayah (that's the Tewa word for grandmother) had no English at all—but there was a true mother-daughter relationship between them."[1] Yet Edith always wanted to somehow capture in words the lifestyle, philosophy, history, culture, and humor of the Native Americans at San Ildefonso. She pounded out page after page of single-spaced writing about the pueblo on her typewriter. Most of her writing had something to do with the village.

Edith's first visit to San Ildefonso was on January 23, 1923, with John Boyd and his son Dick for the dedication of the new plaza. The realignment to the north of the village had occasioned a period of great stress in the pueblo, and disagreements among families had disrupted traditional social and ritual structures. Edith discusses this north-south split, but as Peter observed: "Not only would the village people have been hurt if she had written openly—but she just couldn't have done it."[2] Some of Edith's letters deal with the feuding and alcohol problems at the pueblo. Edith felt strongly that out of respect for traditions that are passed on through generations visually and orally, not everything can or should be revealed in writing.

Relaxing for Health
From Philosophy of Health, *June 1925*

A clever advertising man is awake to the fact that Americans need to stop now and then in the great race of life, and relax. In a recent daily paper the following sentence was part of an advertisement for a restaurant: "Relax at lunch time, for your health's sake."

Picture the noon hour: Men and women hastily donning coats and hats; dashing to the elevators, with bodies tense and minds in a whirl; rushing into a near-by cafeteria or restaurant; ordering a sandwich, pie, and coffee; chewing rapidly, with bodies still tense and minds racing; then hastening to shopping or appointments—and all that to be accomplished in sixty minutes! Could there be a more vicious circle, as far as health is concerned, than wrong food combinations, tense bodies, whirling brains? It would be time well spent if, from half an hour of watching the public eat lunch, one realized how the majority live, and began to look for similar evidences of tension in oneself.

Some years ago a Scotch physician, well trained in the reading of countenances, said: "You Americans wear too much expression on your faces. You live like an army with all its reserves engaged in action. You take too intensely the trivial moments of life." And since that time we have entered the age of speed!

After lunch, the majority rush back to desk or machine, and try to concentrate on the task before them. A certain number of letters must be written, so many dozen shirts must be stitched, before the hands of the clock reach the hour of release. Could the muscles of this large proportion of our population be examined, what would be found? Undoubtedly there would be few exceptions. We should see pen or pencil held as though it might escape; tense shoulders bent over typewriters or machines—doing work that requires only arm and finger muscles; bodies held in the chair as though the chair would not support the entire weight. In the brains atop those tense bodies we should find taut nerves—a mass of hurry, worry, no time, breathlessness.

Days are too short for all the work, the reading, the exercise, the recreation, that we Americans want to accomplish; so we spend them dashing through all that possibly can be done; fretting and fuming about the things for which we have no time; hurrying to bed and to sleep—in order to be ready for another day—without relaxing out of that whirl. What is the result? We go from one physician to another; we endure innumerable treatments; we spend months and money in all sorts of hospitals and sanitariums. Few, if any, of those to whom we go for relief and guidance tell us how to live.

We are prone to look with disdain or disgust upon the Mexican who in the summer leans against the shady side of his adobe house, and in the winter against the sunny side; not realizing that we might learn a valuable lesson in the land of mañana—the tomorrow that never comes. An Irishman living in that land of *poco tiempo*—"pretty soon"—has taken it for his own. Nothing excites him, and his usual reply to any hurrying mortal is: "You have all the time there is, you know, and there is no need of rushing."

Nature's way is ever before us, but we do not read as we walk. Ruskin said: "Are not the elements of ease on the face of the greatest works of creation? Do they not say, not there has been a great *effort* here, but there has been a great *power* here?" There is a canyon in the Jemez Mountains that typifies nature's constant, but slowly evolving, processes. One ascends to a point where the canyon walls seem to meet, goes a few steps around a jutting rock, and finds oneself on a narrow trail that clings to the side of the canyon. Far below is the tiny stream that has carved its way, during many a century, down through the wall, to lay bare to eyes that can read the story of the ages. High above are the huge rocks that were tumbled down, as though by some giant hand, upon the work of centuries. Layer upon layer, stratum above stratum, disclose the history of the earth. How many years were in the depositing of those few inches of yellow sand? How many in its sister-strata? There was no haste there, where reds, yellows, grays, shades never named, are blended—just the unceasing, quiet carrying-out of a plan. Sailing with outspread wings, a bit of black against the deep blue of the sky between the canyon walls, one is apt to see a hawk. There is motion; there is constant evolution; there is steady force; but there is not a hint of haste, of speed, of rushing.

How can one overcome this habit? How can we learn to relax? The first step is to develop an awareness of tense muscles. In exercising, relax every muscle not being used for the particular movement.

When riding, when hearing a lecture, when seeing a movie, relax the tense shoulder muscles. Let the chair do its full duty without human assistance. Relax a few minutes before a meal is begun, and eat less. Before going to sleep, relax each muscle from the toes to the hips, from the finger-tips to the shoulders, from the end of the spine to the head. Relax systematically until the bed bears the entire weight of the body, and the mind, too, has "let go." When the mind is a whirl of circling thoughts, think of some quiet scene—a mirror-like lake, the skyline of a mountain range, the hush of a deep canyon. Relax until it has become a habit.

These are but glimpses into a quiet land—hints of how one may gain entrance to it. Beyond are health and happiness—when one has learned how really to live.

My Neighbors, The Pueblo Indians

From Neighborhood, A Settlement Quarterly, *June 1931*

New Mexico is
A land of sunlight and shadow
Where Indians dance for rain,
And clean winds blow from purple peaks
Down to the cactused plain;
A land of music and silence
And the tom-tom's low refrain,
Where he to whom the vastness speaks
Must stay or come again.

And so when I came almost a decade ago, seeking rest for a weary body and brain, the land of mañana claimed me for its own. For more than a year I lay on the warm earth, rode and walked the trails, began to know the people. And when I had to go away, I knew that some-day I would come back to stay. Cities with their noises and people thronging were scarcely endurable, and always there was the pulling force of this land. So at last I came again when the aspens made great splotches of gold on the mountains, came to stay always. All through the fall and winter I sought a corner to make my own, in which I might eke out an existence. And when the cottonwoods began to leaf, I came here where the Rio Grande enters the canyon made by the great mesas that guard me.

Beyond my mesas to the west are more and more mesas with canyons cut between and behind them are the mountains where the storm clouds gather. Across the river the sun comes up over the Sangre de Cristos, those mountains that change with each hour from sombrest hues to the blood red which gave them their name, to look down on carved marls, which, catching all light and color,

are ever things of beauty, and the peaceful valley. Where there is water in the acequias for the thirsty land, it yields well for Mexican and Indian farmers the native chili, vegetables, fruits, grains, alfalfa, with cottonwoods marking the course of the ditches and the river. And even on the untilled land bloom chamisa and cactus! Through the valley from the east winds the road from Santa Fe with tourists crossing my bridge to seek Pueblo ruins and cliff dwellings, Mexicans and Indians on horseback, in covered wagons, in Fords old and new, driving cattle or sheep, taking beans to plant on mountain ranchitos, going to mass or a *baile*. From out the canyon once a day, a whistle shrieks above the rush of the river, the narrow gauge leaving supplies and guests at my door as it puffs on its way northward.

Were it not for these evidences of it, and the occasional airplane overhead, I could almost forget civilization. The rural route comes only to my nearest neighbor's ranch, a mile away. A telephone is impossible. Water is drawn up from a well. Fireplaces heat my house and candles light it. Nor would I have it otherwise!

Here between railroad and river, with the road not far from my door, I made a crude frame house my home and began my business career with a gas tank, a few candies, "Tobaca Dukey" and some Indian pottery. Three years have added an adobe guest house, known as a place where one finds peace and beauty, and a tearoom which is informally conducted. All of which has helped to send my roots deep, until now I belong here "where the river makes a noise." And when one of the Indian men teasingly asks me when I am going away, I tell him that time will never come, I hope.

Up from the bank of the river several miles to the north rises a mesa called Huérfano or Orphan by the Mexicans, since it stands alone, the Black Mesa by the whites. For miles it dominates the valley and is a constant reminder of the Spanish who came conquering three centuries ago. For there they besieged the Indians, who were secure on its summit because of a secret trail down to the river. To those who know it, the Mesa is still a refuge, a place of peace. And not far away, where the security of the Mesa can ever be felt, live my neighbors, a group of Pueblo Indians.

Around a square plaza they have built their houses of the earth, adobe bricks dried in the sun and laid one upon another, protected by more earth plastered over all by the hands of the women. Pueblo houses vary as do the people, and change, too, as world forces touch and influence their builders. But the great cottonwood which dominates the north plaza, and the old round kiva in the south plaza are marked only by age. They have watched the dances that preceded the going forth of the men to pursue the then thieving Navajos; later, the coming of the encroaching Mexicans, and now, the honking cars that announce the curious and the interested tourists. They have seen the brown babies who played in their shadows learn the songs and the steps of the ceremonial dances, loiter by on their way to the day school, come and go each year to the government boarding school, return to adjust themselves to the Pueblo life and be Indians, or go away to lose their identity in the whirl of a city. White buckskin booted feet still carry water past them, and the beat of the *tombé* and the rhythm of the song is in their ears as in the past, but much of the old has gone forever into that past, customs that were of the earth as are the houses and as essential as the roots of the cottonwood.

There, where their old men predicted the present and were troubled, a gentle people, with a natural dignity, a sense of humor and a philosophy evolved through the centuries, till their fields, make pottery that is art, put their dance figures on paper in paint and ink, carry on some of their ancient customs, and cope, as best they can, with modern conditions. These are my neighbors.

Their acceptance of me has been so gradual through these three years that I can scarcely mark its progress, and yet there are certain steps that stand out. True, I did not come as an entire stranger, for years ago I was taken to several homes in the Pueblo by a mutual friend, and accepted for that reason. But to most of them I was scarcely known, a white woman come to live on their reservation two miles from the village. When I am invited to come into the kitchen, or the inner family room, I know I am counted a friend. And if, when I chance to visit a home at mealtime, an extra cup and plate are placed and I am asked to share the meal, I know I am, as Quebi said, "one of us." Sometimes it has seemed slow progress where natural contacts are few, but when friendship is given, it is not a passing thing. Now I am greeted in Tewa, sometimes followed by "you haven't been here for so long!"

Always have I wanted a home that might be open house to my friends, and from the very beginning of this crude one, folks have come in at the kitchen door, opened to the sun and the song of the river. Uh-de and O-pah-mu-nu were the first in those days when I served tea on a packing-box table, and since that rainy afternoon many a friendly word has passed over a cup of *café* or tea. The many-windowed living room, with its gay rugs, pictures, books and magazines, has known some guests well, others less intimately. It is a room to relax in and the former sit back and enjoy it for hours at a time. Sunday is frequently "at home" day and no unusual sight is a wagon or a car crossing the bridge with gay-shawled women, bright-shirted men and black-eyed children come to visit. Sometimes there is a friendly silence, sometimes animated conversation, but always magazines and papers are scanned. Many weighty matters have been discussed under its rough board ceiling and much laughter has there been by sunlight and candlelight.

Holidays and birthdays are reason enough for one family or another around the long table, with all the special things that most folks enjoy. Sometimes it is just a fireside meal, with songs and tale-telling for dessert, and I find myself enjoying most my Pueblo guests, in spite of conversational lapses into Tewa. And sometimes the men move the furniture, bring two hollow-log drums, and we dance to the beat of the *tombé* and the clear-voiced song of the drummers. Babies fall asleep to the familiar music and are laid on a bed. Children run in and out, or dance, too, but are seldom in the way or misbehaved. And we grown-ups forget all else and dance together, young and old. Being accustomed now to unexpected guests, I am not perturbed, but glad, when along the road comes a familiar blanketed figure. There is always food, should our meal be finished, and somehow I am never too busy to prepare it for Ci-ya-pe. Sometimes there are two, one bent with a stout stick in a brown hand, a battered black hat on the thin graying hair, the "Old One" from Nambe, come walking to see me and to eat in my house. That is an honor.

Always in the Pueblo there is an extra cup of coffee in the pot for me, a tortilla or *bua* in the basket, and I find it a real pleasure to share those meals, especially if they are eaten in Indian fashion. No matter how little or much, it is willingly shared. One day I could stay just a few minutes and Kun-povi may have felt reluctance in offering me their supper, but she handed me a cup of water, making me in that way share the meal. I wonder if she sensed how much that tin of cold water meant to me!

The fireplace is the center of a home in this country and it is always there the chairs are drawn after a meal, and to it a guest is invited to come. At first I formally sat on a chair, but now I feel free to do as instinct bids me, and sit on a low stool or the hearth. I really like to, and then it tends to break down any barriers of difference that might seem to exist. Somehow they stand out in my living here, those fireside hours. One was in an inner room on an evening when the men were busy and we women talked about the babies and our-selves, as women always have, and knew each other better. One was serious talk of the old order changing, with my hostess urging me to spend the night; one such fascinating tale I scarcely could leave. And on one never-to-be-forgotten night, I walked to the village in the moonlight to sit on the floor beside the fire while the Old One

sang songs for me until midnight. About six words I understood, but I needed no language to feel the charm of his thin, but still musical, voice, and the twinkling eyes in his expressive face.

Such kindly thoughtful things they have done. In the beginning when I was tenderfoot enough to think I could raise vegetables with no acequia for irrigation, it was he whom I call Padre who came to plough my garden. I was his daughter, he said, and he did it gladly for me. He has never been too busy or tired to hear my trou-bles and give advice or comfort. And didn't he go hunting an herb to make well my sick knee? It was Uncle John who, seeing me gathering some sticks along the river-bank, thought I needed wood and came bringing a load. It is his needle that mends my moccasins, with never a time of payment, and always he greets me with a cheery, "What can I do for you today?"

In those early days when I was much alone, Ci-ya-pe came often to see if I was "all right," and when the wild winds of that first spring blew so, it was great relief to have him sitting calmly smoking while the little old house shook and shuddered. There had never been any tangible evidence of the understanding between us until one day he called me aside and handed me five dollars. When I looked questioningly at him, his reply was, "You said you were very poor," and it was likely all he had.

One other has come often to see how things went with me or if I needed something, and when Nana-tsideh's white horse comes trotting across the bridge, all the hard and the glad things kept for his understanding ear come to the surface. There is always some door or window to be fixed, a tree planted, a chair mended. And when I have to get away from all of civilization, it is two horses he brings to take me up on the mesas where clean winds blow and there is only silence and sunshine. Sometimes it is Oqua-pi's horse, and I know now that I can never pay in coin for my rides on Lady's back. And Po-sta's voice was sincere when it rang out above the children's prattle. "How did you like my horse? Here he is, use him whenever you want to."

And quiet Uh-de! Not a word spoken, but something done for my comfort to be discovered after he has gone. It is "Anything you want from town?" or "Who's going to take you home?" on a trip to the Pueblo. One summer evening I said I was walking, as I sometimes do, and quick as the flash in his eye came the answer, "Not in those shoes!"

The women have less leisure, they, the mothers and pottery makers, but none the less is their thought of me. Always they are gracious, with interest in all the little things happening to me, and many are the kindly things they do for me. Knowing my special liking for the paperbread of blue corn meal that only the older women make now, O-ne-a-po-vi always saves some for me. If there is *bu-sti-a,* a sweet bread, in the bread jar, Cah-i, remembering, adds

it to the basket when I chance to be there at mealtime; kindly Cah-i, who is wife to my Padre. Rhubarb and carrots and corn from her garden brings O-mah-wi, who calls me sister. Ah-pa, coming to wash or clean, sometimes climbs down from the wagon seat a bit awkwardly, and I know there is something hidden under her red shawl. It has been beets, tomatoes, a melon, blue cornmeal of her own grinding, once some of her pig's backbone. It was Sahn-povi who sent me venison, no small gift even here, and A-goya a box of wild plums, little things so hard to pick, for jelly. And one day Sangh-wah invited me to dinner. It was a meal prepared specially for me, corn cooked in an Indian way, which I had long wanted to taste, *kapowano,* the fried bread I so much like, Indian pie, and celery, because I am a white woman.

Borrowing and lending may be scorned by some, but to me they are part of being neighborly. How could I ever have enough cups for the whole village when we have a *pahn-shadi,* a dance, over here? So Quebi always brings hers, and the big feast-day coffeepot. And my benches always go to the Pueblo for feast days. It is Quebi's pink shawl I wear when I watch a sunrise ceremony, and her bed I share. And when I go to a costume party as a Pueblo woman, the best clothes of the village are at my disposal. One Thanksgiving Day I was arrayed in much splendor, Po-te's silk dress and *ah-hi;* Quebi's silk *muto;* Sangh-wah's best shawl, O-mah-wi's buckskin boots; much silver and turquoise loaned me by all. And Tsah-pa's contribution was bangs for my wig made from his horse's black tail! Even the children are loaned to me, and my happiest hours are when I am free to play with them.

Sometimes they spend a night with me, sometimes a whole wagonload comes and there is much romping in and out of the little old house.

But there is more than all this. I recall vividly a morning when I was ill. The Pino family came in the wagon to see me and sat solemnly while I tried to talk in spite of pain. When they left, grand-mother Sayah who had watched me all through the hour put her arms around me and wept, fearing I might die. We can speak to each other only in the few Tewa words I know, dear old Sayah and I, but that is no barrier and her arms are a haven when I need human comfort. It was after Povi let me put hot compresses on her knee that I felt nearer that diffident lovely woman, and her death touched me as it did the whole village, with whom I wept. Quebi is like a sister and I am glad her betrothal and wedding were my first such experience. They were real ceremonies, and even though I could not understand the words, the depth of it all gripped me and I knew she wanted me to share it as much as I could.

When a certain mood is on me, it is to Sangh-wah I want to go. There is some bond that has no name between us. It makes me feel close to her, and is undoubtedly the reason for the gifts of value to her and me which she has given me. But when there are personal problems to solve, or things in the village worry me, it is to Povi-cah I go to [for] counsel, she whom I count one of the finest of women and feel it an honor to hold as friend. Her confidence in me is held as a trust, and whether it be a house to build, or a misunderstanding to mend, she has never failed me. I told her once as I chanced to meet her in the village that I had something to talk over with her when I could come to see her. The next day she left her work, and she is a pottery maker of fame, to come over here. She thought I was worried and so she came to help me if she could, and she did!

All this is neighborliness in the land of mañana. It matters not that the color of skin be different, that language be not the same, that even the gods of our fathers be known by a different name. We are people, the same kind of human beings who live and love and go on, and I find myself ever forgetting that my friends are known as Indians and I am a white woman born. Perhaps that is why we are neighbors, even down in our hearts.

Cañon People

From Space, *September 1934*

There are more than hill people and plains people and sea people. I decided that last night. There are cañon people. Last night I decided, too, that it was a damnable thing to be—for cañons are so deep and dark and captorlike. Tonight I know that were there no cañons, there could be no mesas where the sky stretches a boundless blue above, the sun shines, the clean winds blow, and the far horizon never limits him who wanders there. Where was the trail by which I climbed from cañon to mesa, I know not. Perhaps the gods lent me eagle wings! Someday I may learn, but just now it matters only that somehow I can go from cañon to mesa—knowing both.

It may have been their calling me through the years that made me so determined, for no good reason, to come to this cañon and mesa country seeking rest for a weary body; and finally to return to live always in the shadow of these great mesas—Shumo-ayde and To-tavi-kadi, Tomo and Tuyo. For it is here my roots have gone deep, and while the land can never be mine legally, being part of a Pueblo Indian reservation, it *is* mine because it claimed me for its own.

But I had never realized before how truly I was just that—a cañon person. It was this way. I wanted yesterday afternoon to go into the sun-warmed outdoors and let the quiet strength of the mesa fill me and the song of the river calm me. Instead I read the paper and balanced my books for the month. No further explanation is needed. Then Nana Tsideh, the past-middle-age Indian who takes care of things generally for me, did not come right back from the community ditch digging in the Pueblo, so that he was not here when the train arrived and express had to be unloaded. It was not a great offense in itself but, coupled with my work's being neglected during these weeks of digging or done by myself, it was the last straw. Even here in this peaceful and beautiful valley, there was the financial problem and the human one, and neither seemed worth solving when my body was aching and my mind circling.

In the evening Nana Tsideh told me there was to be a ceremonial dance in the Pueblo and explained how the women gave gifts of flour and cornmeal to the dancing men and they gifts of cloth to the women. He told me, too, that they liked it when I sent my basket of fruit and cake for the dancers' dinner. (Pueblo women at noon carry bowls of stew and baskets of bread to the kiva for the dancers.) And when I replied that they never told me so or thanked me, he said, "But before they eat and when they dance, they think a prayer for you—that you live long and be happy." So I got ready the basket and my gift of cigarettes for the dancers, and we talked out and solved our labor question.

The dance was to begin at sunrise and Nana Tsideh wanted me to see it then. He had planned to do his work before he went, but I was to go early. When the morning star was bright above the moun-

tains, he built a fire and called me. Through the hush of the dawn I went to the Pueblo. Just as I entered the plaza, the door of the Ceremonial House opened and a blanketed figure came through it, followed by the ten dancers scattering the sacred meal.

The large plaza was still and unpeopled—and I pressed close against the wall of an adobe house as they faced south and began the low song to which moccasined feet beat the earth with the lifted step that seems to take into the dancer strength from the mother earth. Bodies painted black with white circles and spots I saw, red yarn fluttering on legs that moved in unison, embroidered ceremonial kirtles and dangling fox skins, great collars of the sacred spruce, gay feathers dancing on black hair—and familiar faces intent on the prayer-song. All that my eyes saw, bit by bit, while the rich low tones of the song and the rhythm of the movement filled me. From the earth itself and from the house made from the earth it flowed into me—and I can find no word for *it*.

As the dancers faced the east and the blanketed leader called to the earth spirits within the center of their universe around which they were dancing, the sun rose. My eyes lifted from those dancing figures to carved mesas and snow-covered far Tsacoma—the sacred mountain. On all rested the first light of the sun. To the sun, the life-giver, that song seemed to go and into the plaza the sun-power to come—into those bodies so concentrated on the prayer.

And then from out of the house against which I leaned came that old one whom I call Sayah, which is grandmother. I bent to her embrace with that feeling of almost awe which I experience when I realize her faith and love for me. We have only the few Tewa and Spanish words I know, but there is between us an understanding that needs few words. I had not seen her for several weeks, and she had been ill, which made it not an ordinary greeting, and I was much aware of what she meant to me as I turned again to watch the dancers.

Until they had completed the square and filed back into the Ceremonial House I watched, and then went in to warm myself by Sayah's fire. In silence we stood there, her hand in mine. In my memory that dance will always be associated with Sayah, and in that region where we are and have our being the earth-feeling which came to me from the dance and its background will be mingled with that which came to me from her.[3]

Christmas Eve in an Indian Pueblo

From the New Mexico Sentinel, *December 22, 1937*

I

Even here on a Pueblo Indian reservation the approaching Christmas is ruffling the calm that follows corn harvest and wood-gathering. Soon I will go to the hills for evergreens to send to those city dwellers who love this land. Now I am wrapping the Christmas greetings that go to my neighbors in the Pueblo—young and old.

As I worked today, I recalled other years with just such preparation and the climax, Christmas Eve. It must have been my second Christmas, here by the Rio Grande, that Quebi came for me in Awa's car just at dusk. When we reached the Pueblo, little pitch fires were burning in front of every house. By their light we delivered the gifts and then hurried with all the people to the schoolhouse. The room was bright with the gift-hung tree and the shawls of the women, and I drew back into the corner, being the only Anglo save the teacher. The "pieces" and the songs were those eastern children sing; but little Indian tongues did not always get the words of "Merry, Merry, Merry Christmas Bells" and "Silent Night." Nonetheless, their eyes beamed and their clear voices never missed a note.

There were gifts for everyone, from a washtub for Povi-te to a tiny war bonnet for Co-ha. A live turkey in a red wrapping caused much merriment and more when it was handed to me. With the last gift, each mother spread a shawl and the family's share was heaped in it and lifted to the father's back. Then suddenly, like tumbleweeds before a winter wind, all were gone—to open the mysterious packages beside the home fireplace.

Perhaps Povi-stah had pity on my childless estate when she asked me to go home with them. Pineknots soon made a bright light for the presents, and the children opened their packages and exclaimed with delight. Brownie held up corduroy pants and a red sweater. Little Brownie danced and shouted, "Look, look," with a blonde doll on her arm. Baby Brownie squeezed a rubber burro and squeaked with it. Even I had to open my presents while all admired. Win-ke, father of the Brownies, smiled but shook his head, recalling his boyhood when children were satisfied with an orange and a bag of candy.

The children were keeping eyes open with difficulty when Quebi came to call me. We were going to another Pueblo for midnight mass and on our way we stopped at Bouquet Ranch. As we said our Merry Christmas, over the radio came midnight mass from Holy Trinity in New York. There in that old adobe house, with its relics of the Pojoaque mission, we listened as the organ pealed forth and mass was intoned. Christmas Eve in New York! As we drove on I struggled through the present to visualize it, but a deep blue sky with its myriad stars would not give way to the blazing light of sky-scrapers.

Midnight was near when we entered the plaza, lighted by many fires. Their flames blazed high with a sudden wind and the white front of the little church stood out against the blackness of the night. The bell was calling the people to pray—the only sound in the stillness. Silently and singly blanketed men and women came from their houses to kneel before the altar and return. An hour passed but the priest had not come. Perhaps it would be dawn before he got there and those first hours of a day are very long. Perhaps the people, too, were tired of waiting, for of a sudden there was the sound of sleigh bells. Ever since, sleigh bells have meant for me Indian dancers on Christmas Eve. From the darkness they came into the firelit plaza—men in ceremonial kirtles and two women in white ceremonial dresses with eagle feathers in their hair. We followed them into the church and there, before the Virgin and the Niño in a cradle, they danced an ancient dance. Deep drum tones; the lift and fall of moccasined feet; slow, soft movements of full bosomed women; swift circling of long haired men in an altar's candlelight while the Christ Star rose in the east.

II

Several years passed, and another Christmas Eve approached. When the sun had gone below the rim of the big mesa to the west, and the dusk had begun to come silently from the canyon, Nana Tsideh laid a little hollow square of pitch wood outside the house. He lighted it, saying a prayer for those who draw near mankind on that night—be they Christ Child or gods of darker skin.

Again we took our gifts to the Pueblo and listened while the children sang their Christmas songs. Then, through the still cold moonlight, we drove to San Felipe and waited. Midnight came and went, with now and then the church bell ringing and Indians going into the church to pray. At intervals a drummer and a hunter came from the church to go through the village calling to the people. Through the hours we waited, looking at the church in the moonlight and behind it a mesa carved against the sky. I wanted only to be still and passive to the waves that beat upon me from the air. Then a call came through the clear cold of the first hours of Christmas and I knew that the Buffalo Hunter had gone up into the hills. Again and again it came, each time rending more civilized layers of me until it laid bare something deep and ageless.

So it was that when the time came I went into the old seatless church. Bells tinkled and many men and women and children in ceremonial costume, with bows and arrows, entered to form two long lines beneath the candles. I stood beside the old men who sang the prayer song and knew that this dance before the altar was no sacrilege. The rhythm of the song filled me and held me motionless while they danced and then passed singly to pray at the altar.

There was scarcely time to move against the wall among the women before those others came—Buffalo, Deer, Antelope, Mountain Sheep brought from the hills by the Hunter. Again the chorus was beside me, my shoulder touching one of the blanketed singers in the thronging. From the man and from that earth-made church wall a current flowed into me and only those dancing figures existed. I did not want them ever to stop, but almost before they had gone came other figures in from the moonlight. They were Eagles—eagles who were of the gods to me. Almost I held my breath while they circled and swooped with great wings outspread. Reaching the altar, the last Eagle lifted one wing above it as though in benediction. That, too, seemed as it should be. Then out into the dawn of Christmas they danced, leaving me to bind up those rent layers. But with them I bound up a gift from the gods.

$\mathcal{U}$npublished Essays

A Tenderfoot in New Mexico[1]

[To] Frijoles Canyon, now known as Bandelier National Monument,
I came from Philadelphia as a veritable tenderfoot.

Darkness hid New Mexico as I paced the platform at Lamy, waiting for the little train to Santa Fe, but the stars hung low and brilliant in the midnight sky and the air was crisp and clear. I felt that I
had entered another world. In the morning, during the drive to
Frijoles, it became a certainty.

At that time the road passed through the village of Agua Fria
with its adobe houses and irrigated fields, and descended gradually to the Rio Grande, crossing and recrossing the tracks of the
narrow-gauge Denver and Rio Grande Railroad. To the east were
the Sangre de Cristo Mountains, so called by the Spaniards when
they had been awed by the sunset glow on the snowcapped peaks.
That morning they shone with what seemed to me like great
masses of molten metal far up on their sides. Reluctantly I turned

westward only to find before me the Jemez Mountains. There, too, the first frost had turned the leaves of the aspen trees in the higher elevation.

It seemed a world of gold and green without human habitation. The sand shone in the sunlight and the chamisa had golden blossoms. Only the mesas forming the White Rock Canyon of the Rio Grande were dark and where they parted a shaky wooden bridge crossed the river—marked on the map as Buckman. The ascent to the western mesa, which was part of the Pajarito Plateau, was long and steep and used alike by sheep, cattle and men. From it one looked down into the dark gorge of the river, out across the foothills to Santa Fe and up to the gleaming mountains. The sky completed the circle and to my Eastern eyes even the sky was different—its blue, warm and deep.

There was no hint to an untrained eye that here high above the river a culture had flourished long before the coming of the Spaniards. There was no warning that on the Los Alamos mesa, a few miles to the north and west, a new era was destined to begin. Nor did I dream on that still clear day in early October how this very plateau in the shadow of the Jemez Mountains would affect my own future.

Among tall pine trees on the Frijoles mesa the road ended, for in those days a trail wound down the face of the cliff into the canyon, which—to my astonishment—was the site of a prehistoric Indian ruin. A turn in that dusty trail disclosed the crescent-shaped canyon and, far below, a narrow stream lined with alders as bright as the sunlight. Across the Rito de los Frijoles, the little river of the bean, were the stone ranch house and guest cabins where my life in New Mexico was to begin. Behind them rose the steep south wall with piñon and juniper trees among the boulders and a trail climbing to the mesa.

That trail became my testing ground as each day I climbed a little farther. Later it was the vantage point from which I looked into the canyon and out across the mesas. From it I learned to know the north cliff wall with its weathered face and manmade caves, its carved columns and tent rocks. From it the floor of the canyon clearly showed the pattern of the large community house, long in ruins, and the cleared spaces of the fields where corn and squash had grown.

At the ranch house lunch was ready and I welcomed something familiar in a strange world. Sharing the strawberries from the Rito garden were John Sloan and Robert Henri, artists who summered in Santa Fe. This, too, was a link with an unforetold future, for Henri had put on canvas old Diegito of San Ildefonso and his drum. Later I was to mourn the death of Diegito's son, see his grandson married and hold his great-grandson in my arms.

In this long low room where guests gathered around the fireplace and the table with John and Martha Boyd, host and hostess, began another phase of my education. Here John Boyd—tall, lean, dressed in ranch clothes and forever lighting a pipe—made his tales so vivid and was so perfect a host that guests forgot to pay for lunch until they had started up the trail. He had that lack of time sense which is almost imperative if one is to live easily in this land of mañana. Each late guest was just in time for breakfast. Others smiled with him and forgot to hurry. This was sometimes difficult for Martha Boyd, the thrifty housewife, from whom I later learned many of the things a woman in New Mexico needs to know. In this initial stage I had outdoor knowledge to acquire.

Had I not come in that year of 1922 while the Boyds were at Frijoles, someone else might have lived in the house at Otowi Bridge, just above "where the water makes a noise." Had they not taken me into their hearts, I never should have known the people of San Ildefonso, the Indian Pueblo in the Upper Rio Grande Valley known for its black pottery. Without Father Boyd's tutelage, there could have been no background of understanding.

From the vantage point of the present it becomes clear that those four canyon months brought the first conscious realization of many things. The colors of the lichens on the rocks, the strata of the canyon walls where the Rito tumbled down to the Rio Grande, the blue of the sky and the sunset clouds were a daily accompaniment. The wind in the pines, the high clear notes of the canyon wren, the night calls of the coyote were my music. Beside the lower Rito were wild turkey tracks, on the Ancho Canyon road the huge paw mark of a mountain lion, across the trail hoof prints of a deer. A water ouzel bathed in the cold water of the stream. A hawk sailed high above the canyon. Wherever the sun warmed the earth a tired human body could lie and find sleep.

The tufa bricks of my cabin had sheltered men and women hundreds of years before. Their feet had worn the trail in the lava cap where I climbed to the mesa. Daily I picked up sherds of pottery they had made and used. One of them had carved Avanyu, the plumed serpent, on a rock beside the trail. In the caves of the friable cliff the multiformity of doorways and niches bespoke the individuality of these prehistoric people and made them come alive for me. I could understand the woman who, descending, met John Boyd on the trail and asked him if it would be possible to see the caves at the noon hour when the inhabitants might be eating lunch.

Having this foundation of acquaintance with a small section of the country and its people's past, as well as a feeling for it, the time had come for an introduction to the people of the present. After Christmas, Father Boyd took me in the old topless Ford to San Ildefonso with candy for his friends. Beyond Buckman, which was only a railroad stop and a post office, the road was new to me. It skirted the eastern side of Buckman mesa and climbing gradually from the river topped a rise beyond which lay a magic land. On that day pearl gray clouds floated above snowcapped mountains and cast shadows on the barranca [ravine or gorge], gold and rose in the sunlight. Later from the house by the river I was to know the mesa in all its moods, to see the barranca glow as well as withdraw within itself in somber hue. This I did not even dream as we drove toward the Pueblo and the Black Mesa towering it.

In the south plaza centered by the round kiva and in the north plaza shaded by the old cottonwood, children played, as all children play, and ran to see what we had brought. As a newcomer I could be silent, permitting myself diffident observation while John Boyd talked with his friends. The long rooms with white walls and beamed ceilings had little furniture—a few chairs near the fireplace, a trunk, a long roll against the wall, which served as seat by day and, spread out, as bed by night. These did not hide the beauty of the room's proportions nor detract from its spaciousness and dignity. Even more impressive were the faces of those who sat by the fire. Here, too, I found dignity together with intelligence and humor. Later I came to know these men and women as individuals and some of them to love.

When the Boyds decided to leave the Rito, they asked me to go with them to the new ranch at the foot of Las Conchas in the Jemez. So the pattern continued with anticipation offsetting my disappointment caused by this change, but with an interlude until spring came. However even during that period the unrealized preparation for the future continued.

On a gray February day Father Boyd, Dick and I left Santa Fe expecting to reach Jemez Springs, where some new ranch business was to be transacted. A cold west wind blew across the mesa above La Bajada hill and we watched the clouds apprehensively. Above Bernalillo snow began to fall and only Dick's skill got the car as far as Jemez Pueblo. There, opening the door of his store, Hopah bade us come in out of the storm. We must spend the night there he said and perhaps in the morning it would be possible to go on to Jemez Springs.

Father Boyd suggested that I might be able to sleep at the Indian Service farmer's house. Hopah's reply was, "The farmer's wife is a Mexican." That would not have deterred me but I realized that Hopah was displeased. In addition, I had no inclination to leave the known for the unknown, nor to miss anything interesting, so I made very clear my preference. After supper we were ushered into a room apparently used for guests and storage of Navajo blankets sold at the store. Fragrant piñon wood burned in the corner fireplace, where Hopah joined us. Again I was a listener. Unfortunately most of the conversation has been forgotten, but it must have come finally to the weather and the preceding year of drought that had taken severe toll of cattle and wild animals, as well as decreasing essential crops. Then Hopah spoke and the intensity of his face remains even though the outlines have faded. The never forgotten words were, "Last night we danced in the kiva—every man, woman and child. Our hearts were right. Today the snow came."

In the morning the sun shone, but the snow was too deep to

attempt a canyon road. As we returned to Santa Fe, red cliffs rose from the glistening snow to a cloudless deep blue sky. In this beautiful still world I kept pondering Hopah's words.

April was spent at Anchor Ranch, between Water and Los Alamos canyons, and I began to know that part of the Pajarito Plateau. One warm day the Smithwicks took me on a long horseback trip, which led us down Los Alamos canyon to the house built by Rose Dugan and Madame von Blumenthal—now in ruins and currently known as the Duchess's Castle. It had been built before World War I below the northern rim of Tsankawi mesa and abandoned during the war for one or more of the many rumored reasons. Juan Gonzales was the caretaker but San Ildefonso was too far away for more than an occasional visit. So it had become customary for the few residents of the Plateau to climb through a window, examine the interesting house with its zaguáns [small entrance halls], niches, Indian wall paintings, wicker furniture, and leave with a souvenir. Eventually everything but the walls disappeared, but before that the furniture was taken to San Ildefonso. From there the chaise lounge later found its way to a sunny corner in the house by the river.

After lunch we rode up Otowi Hill, following the old road with its hairpin turns, and up the mesa to Los Alamos Ranch School. In that early year of the school's life, it consisted of the Big House and a number of smaller log houses among tall pine trees. The Jemez peaks, Valle del Caballo and Pajarito formed the background of this peaceful mesa high above the canyons and the valley, with the Sangre de Cristos the eastern skyline. My eyes, weary with looking long and far, suddenly spied, beyond the spring mud, color beside the nurse's house. There in the sun's last rays daffodils were blooming.

On the first of May, having loaded the Paige with the necessities of life, Mother Boyd and me, John Boyd, always an adventurer, began the trek to Vallecitos de las Conchas—little valley of the shell. The last lap of the two days' journey was made in a wagon and we found ourselves in a tiny valley where clearings pushed back fir and aspens. Across the stream huge rocks stood like sentinels near the entrance to a box canyon. Peaks of the Jemez Mountains formed the horizon. In this peaceful valley far off the beaten path, horsemen or sheepherders on burros were the only passersby. They were startled to find us there and perhaps resented our presence, as the wild creatures must have.

After several weeks the first crude shelter was abandoned for tents. A long cabin was built with a corral beside it. Logs were cut and hauled in for the main house. In this setting I worked with Mother Boyd and learned some of the things ranch women need to know. A spring furnished water, but it was on the opposite side of the stream crossed by a narrow footbridge. We wrestled with an old cookstove and an uncertain supply of wood. Food was shipped from Santa Fe to Buckman by freight and hauled from there by wagon up Buckman Hill, across the long mesa, up the mountain slope where fir, spruce and pine crowded the rough road, through groves of aspens, down into the Valle Grande with its faint wagon tracks in the grass. Long-range planning and ingenuity were required to feed hungry men. Fresh fruit and vegetables were rare luxuries and I still remember the apricots brought in a wagon from Jemez Pueblo.

Spring came late and gradually in that high elevation. Spring winds blew, fraying nerves and making sunset the day's goal, for as Mother Boyd, comforting me, would say, "The wind will go down with the sun." But there were compensations. Over the white aspens a shimmer of green began to appear and on those trees touched longest by the sun, shiny green leaves unfolded to dance on their slender stems. Each day the color spread and became a little denser, but never matched the darkness of the evergreens. Following a tiny stream one day I found white violets blooming near its banks and later, on a sunny slope, wild strawberries. In the Valle Grande lambs on wobbly legs filled the air with their bleating. In this land, too, were familiar symbols of spring.

We had no radio and mail came in about once a week, but days were so filled there was no time for loneliness. It took me practically a whole day to go to Jemez Springs on horseback for mail—past Vallecitos de Los Indios, over the long mesa trail, down and down into the canyon past the thick walls of the mission ruin and into the village beside the Jemez river. Those trips were wearisome but they gave me confidence in the country, the people and myself.

A Tenderfoot's Wild Ride

It was necessary for someone to bring a horse from Buckman to Santa Fe and I, not being able to peer into the future, volunteered to make the trip. I looked forward to my ride with mingled feelings of pleasure and regret. It had been almost a month since I had been on a horse and I was glad to ride again, but it was a twenty-mile trip and the road was a strange one. Some forefather of mine had passed on to me a dogged determination to go through with things, though, and I started out bravely enough in the car with Dick one clear March day. Most of the snow had melted and we skidded along to Buckman through the glorious sunshine of New Mexico.

Chucita, the horse I was to ride in to Santa Fe, was well named for he is a little thing. Dick says he looks like a jackrabbit. I had ridden him when my riding days began, some months ago, but after Morgan horses he seemed almost a joke for a grown-up to be riding. I was anxious to be off so as soon as he was saddled, I started, eating my lunch as I went.

To appreciate fully this ride, you must know that I had never been on a horse until five months ago, that I am beyond the flapper age, and that I had never been over this road before. Picture, if you can, Chucita, a small brown and homely horse with a scar on his nose, and me in boots, corduroy breeches, moleskin coat, hat pulled down over my head and the inevitable glasses. We were a queer looking pair, Chucita and I, to go riding through the bright sunshine, but very soon other thoughts claimed my attention.

He had been out on the range all winter and the little grass there has been is not conducive to endurance or speed. All of which was fully impressed upon my mind before we had gone half a mile. He neither could nor would lope for more than two minutes at a time, his trot was so slow and his walk was maddening. Then, too, there were many sand arroyos to pull through and I looked forward to the trail along Pankey's fence. Realization, however, proved how false my hopes had been, for it was all sand and, in desperation, I got off and walked. Of course I walked faster than the horse and my shoulders soon ached from leading him. The sand did not make walking easy and I soon began to get tired and sympathize with my partner in distress. Once more I mounted and once more I got off to walk in disgust. I tried to look at the mesas shining in the sun and the sheep grazing on the hillside, but around in a circle went my thoughts. The time, how many miles I had come, how many more there were, would my horse hold out—all these things were alternated with exclamations to the poor animal. To add to my dismay, when I chanced to look back toward the mesa from which I had come, I saw it was snowing. The sky all around me and in the direction I must go was clear and I breathed a sigh of relief and went on—slowly.

They had said the trail left the fence where the railroad turned up into the hills and at last, after two long hours of alternate riding and walking, I left the interminable fence and started into the unknown. A whistle broke the silence and I turned to see the freight coming at almost my own speed. I could not have the trainmen see me walking so I quickly mounted and urged Chucita to do his utmost. I doubt if those men ever knew how glad I was to see them and how sincere was my answering wave. I had not passed a soul, except two Indians just outside of Buckman, and there are times when almost any human will seem like a long lost friend. After a short distance the road, into which the trail led, left the tracks and wound up a canyon to the mesa. If I had known then how endless that mesa was to be and how many hours it would take to cross it, I wonder what I would have done. The clouds had traveled westward and there was no sign of the kind sun. Every minute I expected to feel snowflakes and I had not a match in my pocket. There was not a house in all those miles and I knew I never could find the road in the storms that blow across the mesas. I got off, sat down by the side of the road, leisurely ate an orange, made up my mind that there was only one sensible thing to do, tightened the cinch and started once more.

With the aid of a juniper branch, I managed to get Chucita into a lope and with the stick and my heels in his ribs kept him loping for perhaps half a mile. After that I had to be satisfied with a trot and then a walk. When I felt he was rested and I had to make some progress or scream, we would lope again. The time that seemed an hour at least was ten minutes by my watch. The snow had hidden the Sangre de Cristos from sight but the gods were good and the clouds above me held their contents. I had no idea how far I was from my destination and the mountains, at whose feet lies Santa Fe, seemed no nearer. I whistled, I sang and I reckon it was fortunate that I was the only being on the whole mesa. Not even cattle were grazing there and the solitude I had been wanting for weeks was mine, but, perverse creature that I am, I could not enjoy it. Who could have?

A sound burst upon my ears but, alas, it was only the handcar speeding down the track with two workmen—leaving me even more alone than before. At each rise I hoped there would be something before me other than the everlasting mesa, but there never was. At last, when I began to wonder if it ever would end or if I had been put under a spell by some evil spirit and doomed to wander forever on that same mesa and on a horse that stretched one's patience to the breaking point, I came to a slight rise. Was I dreaming or was that really smoke rising from a tall stack and were those buildings or a mirage? Time would tell and with renewed courage I rode on even though they were soon lost to sight and I was sure that the road led in the wrong direction. Around several more bends we went and then I knew it was not a mirage but reality. Before long I would be in Santa Fe.

Mr. Boyd had said he would meet me for Chucita was not accustomed to city streets. I looked for him anxiously but I reached the first house and the parting of the ways and not a sign of him did I see. After much deliberation, I decided on the road to the left and, fortunately, it led into San Francisco Street. I had thrown away my stick and my only weapon was my heel. How I wished for spurs! Chucita was wary of every step of the way as we proceeded slowly to the railroad. Still no Mr. Boyd and I knew I never would have courage enough to go through the business section. So I turned off to Water Street. A laundry on the corner and some girls laughing made me realize that the worst part of the journey was before me. Scared to death by every sound was the tired animal. Every time a machine passed us I prepared for the worst but all Chucita did was to lessen speed until we were fairly crawling along. Everyone looked at us in an amused way and it was a veritable running of the gauntlet. Heels kicking his ribs availed nothing and Palace Avenue seemed longer, much longer, than the mesa ever had. Inwardly I shrank from the eyes of every passerby but I forced a smile so that they might perhaps be deceived into thinking I wanted to crawl and was enjoying it. All things come to an end sometime though. I know that no place will ever seem half so desirable as our little house did when I at last rode up to it just five hours and a half after I had left Buckman.

It is now a part of the past—that trip—and time has toned down the details until it has become just another funny incident in my memory of New Mexico. I do not know how others feel about it but to myself I am no longer a tenderfoot.

The Basket Dance

One day word came from Tonita telling us that they were to have the basket dance on Wednesday. We had heard that food was not very plentiful in the Pueblo and this confirmed it, for they usually held the dance later in the spring as it was a prayer for food. Needless to say we went, for there would be few if any white people there and it was a real ceremonial dance.

As we entered the plaza they had just begun. A square was marked by four small cedar trees placed at each corner. On one side of the square stood the dancers—about twenty men, and facing them the same number of women. The men wore the ceremonial kirtles of embroidered cloth with girdles to match and fox skins hanging from their waist in the back. Their faces were painted and to their arms and legs were fastened cedar branches beside the usual rattle at the knee. In their hand they held the gourd rattles that are ceremonial. The women were dressed in dark dresses, even their shawl, which hangs from the shoulder in the back were dark. Only their white boots and the green boughs in their hair made any brightness. Each one carried an Indian basket woven of reed and grasses and in the other hand a branch of cedar.

We left the car and walked over near them just as the women knelt facing the men and rhythmically brushed the bottom of the inverted basket with the cedar. They all chanted the refrain while the leader, wrapped in his blanket and standing in the square, sang the prayer. Always the men dance with a peculiar step. We could not understand the words, but the leader's gesture told us he was asking that the sun shine on the planted seed, the rain fall, the seed grow and bear much grain. It was truly a prayer and a people at worship. There was undoubtedly a supreme being in that plaza, and I felt it was a sacrilege to be watching their worship. I found myself unconsciously bowing my head in recognition of the prayer.

Then the women stood and danced with the men, repeating it in another side of the square. Something drew my attention to a housetop nearby and I saw two men with naked, painted bodies and knew they were the Koshare, which means Delight Makers. Long ago when Moctezuma came, the Koshare appeared, bearing horns of grain, nuts, fruit, and always they have tried to make the people happy. Some of their actions and the painted bodies and faces make us think of clowns, but they are in no sense that. As they came down to the plaza, we saw that they were Ignacio and an old blind man. Such queer-looking creatures they were with their horns and long black tails. After much dancing around Ignacio brought to the leader a pot of coffee and a plate of some kind of bread—bringing food as the first Koshare did. After all the dancers had gone to the kiva the two men sat there in the square and ate the bread and drank the coffee with much evident pleasure. Then they went dancing around to the houses and to us who sat in the plaza singing a song that meant good wishes. Back came the dancers and on each side of the square the dance was repeated.

Dick had happened to catch a fox in his trap that morning, and as only the foot was injured, we took it with us. When Ignacio heard it was a female, he asked to have it, and all afternoon he danced around the line of dancers with the fox in his arms, waving it up and down and singing so happily. The last thing we saw as we drove off was the women kneeling, brushing their baskets, and chanting the refrain while the men danced the same peculiar step.

Do you wonder I become indignant when a Commissioner, who probably never saw a dance, forbids these ceremonial dances? He made an awful mistake, and already he is trying to retract. I wish you, too, could see, for I can't make you see it as I would.[2]

Fiesta Time at San Ildefonso

I wonder if these cliffs that have been reflecting the old sun's rays all through the years know how they calm the ruffled, troubled soul of me? I wonder if the people who lived in these cliff caves so long ago felt as I do the sureness, the timelessness of them and so walked calmly through life. When I come here and sit on the stone worn smooth and a bit hollowed by moccasined feet, with my back against one cliff, so solid and assuring, around me the entrances to caves where people lived, loved and died, my mind clears as do troubled waters when the sand sinks to the bottom of the pool. Perhaps I can make it clear.

Today someone told me of several intelligent American men and women, who, having been privileged to witness a Pueblo Indian ceremonial dance, said, "And they call *that* a dance. Let's go show them what real dancing is." I was infuriated. Somehow while I have been sitting here in the sun, such thoughts have fled and now I am realizing that those people had no background for the dance, no understanding, and I am only sorry that they did not know. Perhaps I can picture to you the dancing of real Americans—although words are so futile.

Fiesta time at the San Ildefonso Pueblo was approaching. Preparations had been going on for weeks and every man, woman and child looked forward to the great day. I, too, had been counting the days, watching the weather and hoping that there would be no spots causing me to miss this great event. The day before, January 22, dawned clear and cold and the morning passed all too slowly. After lunch we got the bedrolls ready, for we were to spend the night in the Pueblo—Mr. Boyd and I. My bathrobe was rolled with the bedding, some handkerchiefs put in my little toilet case, which I left in the car, and we were ready.

At last we were off, climbing the trail in the hot afternoon sun. A car takes one all too quickly through the canyons, over the mesas and down the last long hill to Buckman. From there we went up among the sand hills and on to the spot where I always hold my breath. Yes, there they were—miles and miles of foothills all glistening in the sun, like the celestial land, with snowcapped mountains above them. Sometimes when the world seems a horrid, dismal place, I think I must have dreamed those golden hills. A few more miles, a bend or so and we could see the Black Mesa guarding the little Pueblo at its foot.

As we neared it and entered through the new plaza with its many little piles of pitchwood, my anticipation began to be realization. To a casual onlooker, it was just an Indian and Mexican village of adobe houses—squatty and stupid. To me it was the scene of tales told in front of the fireplace at Frijoles by John Boyd. It meant the people I had known first through him, and then in actuality. It was the concrete form of the Pueblo Indian fabric, which was, and still is, in the process of weaving in my mind.

There was time for visiting before sundown, so we left our bedrolls at Ignacio's and went to see Tonita. We found her sitting at one side of the room, apart from her guests, holding her sick baby in her arms. Such distress as was pictured on that mother's face! Babies so often go, but, as the Indians believe, their souls linger near and enter the body of the next to be born. As we went on to Anna's house, many were entering the Pueblo. There were Mexicans from nearby ranchitos and Indians from other pueblos, coming alone or with their families, on horseback or in wagons. Such color against the later afternoon sky!

At five o'clock the church bell began to toll and here and there a woman hurried to mass. Most of the Indians are nominally Catholics but they have not given up their own religion and to permit this the Catholic church has been wise. The sun had set and we went slowly back to our headquarters, stopping often for greetings. It was good to sit quietly by the fire while Susana and Rosalie prepared our supper. We needed the quiet so that the Fiesta spirit might permeate us. The softly moccasined feet of the women made a soothing sound as they moved to and fro on the adobe floor, setting the table with the usual silver, plates and saucers. We were guests of honor as the table showed.

I did not see or hear a signal but there must have been one, for Susana, taking some coals from the fireplace, hurried out to kindle the pile of pitch in front of the house. As we reached the door, the whole new plaza was lighted by the flaming pitch. No one explained it to us, and we asked no questions but we both felt it was what we would call a dedication of the new plaza. With each new event something gripped me stronger.

As we finished our supper of stew, bread, butter, jam and canned peaches—most of it being served to us only, I know—a young Domingo Indian came in. He told us he was Patricio and when I exclaimed, "You are Witter Bynner's friend," he seized my hand and held it in a firm clasp—unusual for an Indian. When he had eaten, he joined us in the long room which was living room and bedroom. Somewhere he had learned some Hopi songs and sang several for us. Meanwhile two Cochiti Indians and their families had arrived, the three Picuris men had come in from their visiting, and Rosalie was putting her dress on for the rehearsal that was soon to take place in the kiva. At last they had all gone and we sat alone with young Ignacio, who was home from the Indian school for the Fiesta. He seemed not quite an Indian, dressed as he was in the American clothes provided at the school. I liked the pleasant bashful lad and kept hoping all through the next day, as I watched him stand aloof and apart, that soon he could leave the school and come back into the pueblo as one of his own people. I question the wisdom of schools that tend to break down the ancient civilization and give only a smattering of our own.

It was clear and cold and the stars, that seemed so near, lured me out into the night. From the hall on the edge of the pueblo came the music of the Mexican baile—dance. You see, Mexicans long ago came in and built houses on the Indian reservations and now there is more or less friction and trouble. The only evidence of dancers in the old kiva was the smoke rising from several openings, and now and then a low chant. There were lights in many houses and preparations for guests went on. Both plazas were deserted save for us. Beyond, the quiet hills kept watch.

When the rehearsal was over, Rosalie came to prepare the beds. There were fully ten guests in the small house and an American hostess would have been rushing frantically here and there in an attempt to find bed space for them all. Not so with Susana and Rosalie. Very calmly and laughing softly they arranged it all, brought us a plate of shining red apples and went away to cook the food that must be ready in the morning for all who would come.

Then came Ignacio in the garments he had worn in the kiva and sat down with us in front of the fireplace. He was the perfect host, expressing his sorrow that he was so busy, and then giving us an hour of the evening where there was still preparations for him to make. He is not only the Cacique but has certain duties to perform in the church at all masses. Turning to me he said he would tell me the story of the moving of the pueblo, but first he must close the window and the door, for, as he put it, "some Mexican might be around and hear." As he returned he prefaced his story with, "I never tell any Mexican and not all white people." It was a rare privilege that was about to happen to me and I recognized it. I would that you might have been there. No pen can describe the face and the voice, much less the soul that one saw and heard in both, of the Cacique, the leader, the high priest of his people. I sat tense, with my eyes on his face. When he stopped to apologize for his lack of English, I hastened to assure him that I understood and I did. I know he did not want me to repeat the story promiscuously so I can only tell you parts of it.

History repeats itself always and these people, when it was necessary to enlarge their pueblo, refused to follow the advice of the cacique, who had been in the kiva four days praying and "doing his business," which was ceremonial. Some of them, though "they talk good with their mouths, are bad in their hearts," disobeyed and built the new houses in the wrong place. The result was just what the very old, wrinkled and bent, but *very wise* cacique said would happen. As Ignacio explained it, they were like the corn when it grows up and something breaks the stalk. Just as the broken stalk yields no corn and finally dies, so it had been with the people. Instead of flourishing, they weakened and many died until only a few were left. Ignacio's heart was heavy and sad, the heart that as he said, loved all people, not only his family, his pueblo, but all people. I know he does and that he spoke only truth when he said, "When I go into the kiva to do my business and pray, I pray for all—Indian, Mexican, white people." After much fasting and praying on his part, many days spent in the kiva, after much dancing, which is praying, by all the people, they took the advice given long ago by the wise old cacique, and decided to move the pueblo. They had begun to do it. The dance the next day was to be danced in the new plaza and Ignacio was happy for surely now they would prosper and grow. In four years they would know, he said.

From that he went on to the story of the Black Mesa and the fight his people had made against the Spaniards so long ago. The soldiers had surrounded them, thinking it was only a question of time until they would have to surrender. But the Indians knew a trail leading down to the river from this black rock table. In the night they stole down and through the Spanish lines and carried water back to the people on the mesa. Not one of them was killed during the long siege and finally the soldiers left them to occupy in peace the land of their fathers.

Insatiable, I wanted more but there were still duties to perform and he excused himself and left us to a quiet that vibrated with the thrill of the last hour. That was the keynote, the climax of the Fiesta for me and will ever remain in vivid memory, the main design in my Indian fabric.

Left alone for a few minutes, I slipped off my clothes and into my bedroll, which had been spread on the one bedstead—the place of honor. Mr. Boyd's roll had been placed on the floor and, at the other end of the room, those of the three Picuris men. It was not so wild and hardboiled as it sounds but quite sensible and proper. I have learned out here that civilization has disadvantages, and I am grateful to the ancestor from whom I inherited the ability to adapt myself to circumstances and some little common sense. Otherwise I would be most unhappy.

Morning dawned bright and clear. Discovering that all the men had risen and gone out, I scrambled into my clothes. I was lacing my boots—hair down—when one of the Picuris men entered and sat down near me by the fire. He wasn't in the least embarrassed for I was a woman and he had seen his own put on their soft white buckskin boots many times, most likely. He did exhibit a bit of interest when I combed my hair for that was a novelty but with it all he was most silent and polite—with not at all the same mental attitude many of the men of my people would have assumed and made me feel.

Breakfast was not prepared so we wandered through the plaza and out on the road in the early morning. The hills, fantastically carved by wind and water through centuries, were veiled with a new tinge and I worshipped the creator of such wonder. The tolling of the bell called us to mass for the Indians. We entered and took our places in a rear pew, feeling very much out of place and very cold as there was no fire in the building. Officiating with or rather assisting the priest was Ignacio in an American suit. It gave me a queer feeling and I couldn't help wishing that it were someone else. To me he was Cacique. We could not understand a word of the service as it was in Spanish, but we had come especially to see Julianita married to a Zia boy. They sat in the front pew with Juan and Ramona as attendants. White did not seem a fitting bridal gown for an Indian girl and I kept wondering what she had worn when their own ceremony had been performed. When we could stand the cold no longer, we quietly left and hurried back to the fireplace.

After a breakfast of many queer dishes of which I tried only one of rice and raisins, we went visiting. Homes were open, Mexican women assisted in the preparation and serving of food and one ate at all hours. More Indians and Mexicans had arrived in blankets and best clothes and the plazas were gay and festive with the throng. As we entered Juan's house, we found the wedding feast in progress though there was no sign of bride or groom. At a small table in the front room, a Mexican with long, curled moustaches presiding, one drank "pop" from small glasses and ate raisins, cake and candy from colored glass dishes—quite festive I assure you. Everyone came to partake no matter whether they knew the host or not. . . . We went into the next room to find their own feast of more substantial food spread. It had not been long since breakfast, but I ate a piece of Ramona's good cake. Having talked to Juan and Ramona a few minutes, and seeing Abel's beautiful bead vest, we went over to Anna's house. She was not there, and we knew none of the visiting Indians, but we sat down anyhow and while Mr. Boyd talked to the man who could speak English and handed out chewing gum and cigarettes, I made friends with a little six-year-old from Taos who could speak no English. Her father told me her name was Anita and with that we made great progress. Her little hands were not lily white and her teeth spoiled any beauty but her big black eyes were dancing and talking to me and who can resist a youngster leaning against one, wanting some affection? We admired each other's jewelry and played a little game with our hands. I think the Indians were amused and pleased and I had a wonderful time. Later we met again and I have a very poor picture of my new little friend.

About eleven there was music and everyone rushed to the plaza to see the dancers come out of the kiva. There they came, men and women in ceremonial garments and bright dresses and shawls, head-gear of feathers, feathers in their hands and a sort of banner of bright colors. It was the Comanche war dance and rather different from their own both in costume and step. Followed by the chorus of some six men with drums, they wound in a serpentine way to the churchyard and then over to the new plaza. The crowd followed, taking pictures and keeping the poor governor busy. It was a strange and beautiful sight in a stranger setting of wonderfully colored hills and sky, adobe houses with figures wrapped in bright blankets on the rooftops. The music is unlike anything you have ever heard—not even the scale is the same. After perhaps half an hour of dancing they went back to the kiva to rest, and between each part of the dance one walked about meeting and greeting one's friends. The peasant festivals in Europe are similar, I imagine. Just before the sun set they danced into the kiva and it was over as far as onlookers were concerned. I had seen piles of pitch on the roof of the kiva and had a hunch that if we could have stayed all night, we might have seen the real dance. I was satisfied—muchly so—for the night before had been very real.

My Friend—a Pueblo Indian

I have just come from seeing Sayah (which means grandmother) in the Pueblo on whose reservation edge I live. Sayah and I have been friends for eight years. The first day she came to my house we knew, without even my few words of Spanish and Tewa, that something which is the beginning of friendship. It is not for my few gifts of little value that she loves me—and that love cannot be questioned when she takes my face between her hands and tells me I am her daughter for whom she cares much.

There are, undoubtedly, so-called friendships formed and continued for what Anglo or Indian get out of them. It may be material things, sentimental satisfaction, curiosity, maternalism, an inferiority complex. Usually an Indian is wary where he bestows friendship, although sometimes not wary enough. Sometimes he sembles at friendship, but he is capable of it—that I know.

A man who had lived for years in this Pueblo country asked me dubiously—"Do you think Indians are capable of friendship for an Anglo?" I tried to illustrate my certainty of it by telling him of Ci-ya-pi. I wish I had not, for he could not understand.

Perhaps Ci-ya-pi's friendship for me stands out clearly because I see it in retrospect. So often on quiet Sundays I would see him coming along the road to the bridge, red bandana around graying hair tied in a chongo, hands clasped behind him or holding his blanket against the cold, shoulders a little bent in later years and a stout stick aiding him. If it were not mealtime, I would put on the coffeepot and go to the door to begin the game we always played.

It was not so in those first days when he came to see what manner of white woman had come to live here by the river. He came frequently that summer—talking little and smoking much, for he was a man of few words and fewer friendships. It was a gradual building process and many months passed before I was sure how he regarded me. Then one day he offered me all the money he had because he thought I needed it. Through that first winter and spring, when I was alone and the wind was a fearsome thing to me, he came often to see that I was "all right" and to sit with me. When the wind blows now in the spring, until nerves jump, he seems very near and I feel that he has come to help me be calm.

He was known as a silent man who held himself apart—a watcher. But to me he talked a little of himself and what worried him, and of things he thought during long hours beside his fire. He had, too, the love of fun and laughter that is typical of Pueblo people. (There were several games of his invention that we played through the years—games of words—that never failed to bring laughter.) Sometimes he brought a visitor—the Old One I called him, who was little and bent but with twinkling eyes and full of fun. Together they tried to teach me their language and no teachers ever laughed as much. Once I went to Ci-ya-pi's house and the Old One sang for me, ending each song with his little laugh and a slap on his knee. I like to think of the two sitting there in front of the fire happily and also of them coming together along the river road to see me, whom they called Koon-povi (Corn Flower).

A "sickness" came to Ci-ya-pi following a break in the friendship of the two men. He could no longer smoke and scarcely eat. That he, who would have none of doctors, went once with me to see a doctor was evidence of the bond between us. But it was too late and each time he came he walked more slowly and I took him home. The last time he asked to be brought over for Sunday dinner, he knew it was his farewell and I felt it. After he had eaten, I asked him in Tewa if he had had plenty. That was the last time I saw in his eyes a very individual lighting and lifting that I had learned showed his pleasure. I realize now that teaching me his language was more than fun. It helped to bridge the gulf of racial heritage between us. It was a reaching toward each other that comes in friendship.

The thing that was hardest to bear as I watched him go slowly toward the end was his drawing deep within himself, of being alone and very lonely. I could only touch his cheek or hand to tell him I was there, hoping he knew how I felt, and take the few things he could eat.

One other Sunday found him gone and when I went to his house they had wrapped his body in his blanket and laid it again on the floor. Like him, I was silent but sobs shook me, for I loved him and he had gone. I could only gather apple and wild plum blossoms and go back to watch through the night, counting my memories of him. In the morning they took his body to the church for burial but I could not bear to go. To me he did not belong there. I found myself going sobbing down the road he had followed so many times when he came to see me, aware only of loss, of emptiness. Finally I looked up toward the west and there came like a flash the deep certainty that he had preceded me and gone on to the mountains! I knew he was happy there and, lest I make it difficult for him to do his work, I must not mourn. So I came slowly along the river to my house, where he had liked to sit and smoke, the hereafter touching me closely for the first time.

By afternoon clouds had hidden the clear sky of morning and a gentle rain fell here, as in the Pueblo. My friend had gone but he had sent the rain. Now, when the winds blow, when the rains fall gently, when special days come in the Pueblo, he is very near and I am happily aware of him. Without a vital friendship between us, that could not be.[3]

J O U R N A L S   (1 9 2 9 – 1 9 3 5)

*A*fter searching for years, I finally found out what happened to Edith's famous journal—Edith asked her sister Velma to burn it. Although she found this a very difficult request, Velma kept her sister's wish.[1] A few people had access to the journal before it was destroyed, and wonderful bits and pieces are left. Edith herself edited and typed some excerpts, and Velma gave them to Peggy Pond Church. The literary magazine *Space* printed a few snips.

Peggy Church wrote, "A little of the shadow side of our lives is preserved in these journal entries. . . . Edith . . . long ago discarded the fretful pages that dealt with . . . inner struggles and discontents. The rest has blown away with the chaff, or forms part of the roots of time."[2]

Velma described a vision Edith had, giving us a hint of what else was in the journal and another reason why Edith wound up in a pitched-roof adobe house with wood heat and no running water or electricity:

A house by the side of the road where she could provide rest, peace and a proper diet. I'm sure she didn't know how it was possible or perhaps it was a subconscious seed but surely it was what she succeeded in doing for many plus a spiritual renewal. Her [journal] notebook is full of diet material and impressions while fasting. Curiously enough she returned to the fasting herself at the end which I believe gave her such a clear mind.[3]

I arranged this work chronologically and made minor spelling corrections. This is what survives from Edith's journal.

SEPTEMBER 6, 1929

It is a feast day at San Ildefonso. I am glad, so glad to be alive and here, with the past year of adjustment and illness only a memory. It is a fall day with great clouds, soft breezes from the south—the kind that draws my soul a tiptoe. Perhaps part of the exultant mood is due to what I saw this morning. As I went to the Pueblo I recalled my first September Corn Dance. I had come on horseback from the mountains and stayed over. The babies I had held then were dancing today and from the shade of the big cottonwood I watched them. Just beyond me were the chorus and the dancers with an old two-storied house and the Black Mesa as a background. There were no cars, no curious tourists to mar the solemnity—only Indian children who belonged.

Here where I know each one, it is faces I see; attitude I note; feeling I catch. The words of the song, the gestures of the chorus, the figure of the dance had no literal meaning for me, but I felt the intangible that permeated them. It was not similar to those moments when all of me seems drawn upward by the beauty of the night or the hills. It was more what one might feel in a Presence. And somehow there in that plaza, guarded by the old, old cottonwood, the last dregs were drained from me. I can endure almost anything if now and then come such hours.

OCTOBER 6, 1929

I ran away today, so sick I was of the kitchen and everlasting food. Constant walls and a roof do something to me at any time and when the aspens turn golden, I seethe inside until finally I revolt and leave everything.

The sun was just above Baldy when I walked to the Pueblo for the old white horse, but by the time I reached the trail leading to the top of Shumo, it was halfway up the heavens. Shumo has a round knoll on its mesa top, which is the highest spot in the valley, and I had to be on top of my world today. All the beauty of the valley lay below me. Beyond were mesas reaching westward to the Jemez with its great masses of golden aspens. The whirring of a bird overhead and the rushing of the river far below were the only sounds.

If I were a leader of people, on such a day I would send them alone into the open.

DECEMBER 28, 1929

One learns through the years to stand alone and to find within one's soul most of what one needs. But there are times when the utter aloneness and apartness overshadows all compensations; when all the treasured little things such as Sayah's "my grandchild," Quebi's "I wish you were going too," Oqua's long-ago planned Christmas gift, turn to ashes.

Nana would tell me at such a time to say a prayer and sing, forgetting myself.

JANUARY 2, 1930

I have been sitting here looking at the peaked ceiling of two grey, one brown, one rough and one smooth board—the only roof for which I have any affection, and wondering why such heights and such depths have been given me. There are days when I question the gods. And then come the things that make me catch my breath. There are moments when this crude house, my little pottery singing-woman, my books and pictures are filled with something living that sends out to me peace. Is it because of an ancient prayer that color and form and movement have come to mean so much more, or is it that the years bring an increased vision—no, a more understanding vision? Is it a natural growth that accompanies maturity, or is it a gift of the gods?

JANUARY 6, 1930

My eyes are still seeing dancers, my ears still hearing the beat of the *tombé* and the rise and fall of voices. I should not have left whatever business there might have been, but when Awa asked me to go to Santa Clara this morning I locked the door, and went. I needed it.

Always the eagle dance fills me with something of the sky. Today I watched the dancers from such close proximity that I saw leg muscles move. As I watched, oblivious of chorus and onlookers, there came something of the gods to those hovering, circling eagles. Then from a housetop I looked down at the whirling, swooping dancers and into the heights they took me—up where the god-powers dwell. That was a dance for the soul.

But what a feast for the eye was the Hopi belt weaving. I told Quebi that if I were an Indian, I would want to be a man, to dance as the men do. My body still seems to whirl and turn with them. But as I watch it in memory, the dance revolves around the women— the women who softly, lightly, slowly, with feet scarcely lifted from the ground, form the center of the movement. Pueblo women are

like that—soft laughter, low voices, quiet steady movements, holding their men and their children through the life dance. But it was the men I watched intently—those Hopi men who danced in and out and under with supple bodies turning, twisting; heads upflung; feet touching earth so lightly; weaving, winding, unwinding, dashing and darting. Still I see them, beaded moccasins that housed winged feet; bodies where dwelt swift winds.

JANUARY 19, 1930

Twice within this week have I seen what must be meant only for the delight of the gods. I chanced to look up from my reading a bit ago and went flying to the riverbank. My carved foothill, which is now just a little more colorful than the others, was a shining thing of beauty. No artist could capture the gold that bathed it with wonder and set it apart. And while I looked in awe, from its earth-hold rose slowly a new color—a cloak of mauve only less bright than the gold that with a caressing movement wrapped itself about my golden hill. Only then could I look up to faraway purple mountains and the Mesa which was quite black against a clouded sky. When I looked back to the hill, the magic was gone. Can such beauty be, and then not be? I think the gods must have taken back to themselves that godmade color—perhaps to paint themselves for an approaching ceremony. And I know that some of it came to stay with me.

FEBRUARY 3, 1930

Again the snow. It came with the night, and when I went to the door a minute ago, it was still falling softly and steadily. Evidently it does not bother owls for one of them hooted at me just as I opened the door. I have my suspicions about that owl and fired the gun to let him know. Povi told me once that she heard an old man scolding a suspicious owl. If it were not snowing, I think I would go out and talk to this one.

FEBRUARY 10, 1930

Across the river the steam shovel with its giant arm eats all day the hill beside the road so that cars can go touristing on their way without difficulty. From here it goes to dig out the side of Ancho Canyon and then Frijoles. No more will mountain lions stalk the colts in the hush of Ancho, nor I climb out of Frijoles where Indians wore deep steps in the rock. I am glad I knew it all when there were only trails and the beauty still held peace.

MARCH 2, 1930

This morning when I stood on the riverbank, the sun was making all golden the edge of the clouds in the east. There was blue sky above Shumo but snowflakes were blown thick and fast from the canyon until they hid the mesas. As they shut out the world and made for me a hushed place in their midst, I was very near the source of things.

FEBRUARY 1933

The winds tried hard yesterday to blow away the snowfilled clouds, as they have for weeks, but finally with a last great blast they went back to their caves and were still. All night and all day the clouds have hung low and refused to let the sun shine through rifts for long. And from them have come rain and hail and snow to the thirsty earth. I had forgotten that snowflakes could fall so gently to make a curtain that shuts out the world. Perhaps never before had I known snow like this, for the Pueblo people have been calling it to come. Today they are dancing the Turtle dance—all the men and boys in ceremonial costume with gourd rattles to mark the rhythm of the song. It is a long song that calls the rain to come and the earth to yield—the same that those ancients prayed when they lived in canyons and on mesas. And perhaps, then as today, the snow fell in such stillness to the waiting earth. It seemed as though the gods came in the sky as great eagles who gave the soft white down from their breasts. It was in the hair of the dancers and on the breast of the earth—sent by the gods to those who forget not how to ask for it.[4]

FEBRUARY 1933

This afternoon as I ironed I was thinking about money. Unexpectedly during the week enough had come in to pay a bill that I did not see how I could meet. I recalled how frequently that had happened when I had done what seemed to be my utmost. I recalled, too, how a wise old man had taught me not to worry about such things. But habit is strong, nor have I learned to live as simply as he. Yet each year I do less of the customary things of our civilization.

Then as I worked, thinking of such things, there came without warning a flowing into me of that which I have come to associate with the gods. I went to the open door and looked up at the mesas with something akin to awe. It forced me out into the open where I could look up to those high places on which humans do not dwell. Then it left me—perhaps to return to those sacred places.

MARCH 2, 1933

This is a day when life and the world seem to be standing still; only time and the river flowing past the mesas. I cannot work. I go out into the sunshine to sit receptively for what there is in this stillness and calm. I am keenly aware that there is something. Just now it seemed to flow in a rhythm around me and then to enter me— that something which comes in a hushed inflowing. All of me is still and yet alert, ready to become a part of this wave that laps the shore on which I sit. Somehow I have no desire to name it or understand. It is enough that I should feel and be of it in moments such as this. And most of the hatred and illwill—the strained feeling is gone—I know not how. (I learned later of the Los Angeles earthquake.)

APRIL 14, 1933 GOOD FRIDAY

Yesterday when I woke there were clouds in the east and I was happy. Later the winds blew them away and I doubted. But by noon the snow had come and it fell until the earth was thickly covered. When darkness came, I went out into it—that softly falling whiteness in the hush of the night. This morning all was heavy with snow and from it rose a white veil about the foot of the Mesa. I was alone in a world of snow and I was conscious only of what came to me from it.

MAY 21, 1933

No, it is not what [Russian writer P. D.] Ouspensky experienced when he was drawn by the waves into them, becoming all—mountain, sea, sky, ship. I am I and earth is earth—mesa, sky, wind, rushing river. Each is an entity but the essence of the earth flows into me—perhaps of me into the earth. And to me it is more than a few seconds' experience. Nor is it any longer strange but natural, not ecstatic but satisfying. The detail of life becomes the scaffolding.

JUNE 1, 1933

I was thinking as I washed dishes this morning. When I had a tooth extracted a few days ago, I was very calm. As I sat in the chair, I saw inwardly my mesas. From thought of them strength and calm seemed to come to me. I became tense at times, but as soon as I thought of them, I relaxed. It was not that the fear ceased to exist, and now the pain, but that another thought was greater than me.

That must explain what M said. She felt a fear that I did, but she said, "I am strong in my heart." Surely that is saner than saying there is no fear, no pain.

When I cease this seemingly endless activity and am quiet, all that is about me comes crowding, and I desire most to remain so until I can let it fill me.

JUNE 25, 1933

But Mr. F. was wrong yesterday when he said that this country was so old it did not matter what we Anglos did here. What we do anywhere matters, but especially here. It matters very much. Mesas and mountains, rivers and

trees, winds and rains are as sensitive to the actions and thoughts of humans as we are to their forces. They take into themselves what we give off, and give it out again. I wonder if it was my hatred and fear that turned the cedars brown and if the tumbleweeds are my thoughts of some people.

I am glad that the years of adjustment are over, and that there has come to me this new relationship with all of earth. I know that I was never so aware of the river and the trees; that I never walked looking so eagerly for the new wild things growing. I know that I have had to grow sufficiently—no, to cast off enough of civilization's shackles, so that the earth-spirit could reach me.

OCTOBER 10, 1933

From every window I see golden trees swaying in the gentle winds and I find it hard to decide whether they are more beautiful in sunlight or in shadow. It is a time to go silently, lest a spoken word break the rhythm.[5]

OCTOBER 11, 1933

Today two men were here from the east. They wondered which landscape I preferred, and wondered more when I declared this was my choice. And when I said I felt this was a more intimate country, they probably thought me very queer. I have been lying here, looking out at the mesa, and the aspens, all golden on the Sangres, and I know that no wooded, verdant country could make me feel as this one does. Its very nudity makes it intimate. There are only the shadows to cover its bareness—and the snow that lies in them late in the spring. I think I could not bear again masses of growing things, great trees, thick undergrowth. It would stifle me, as buildings do.

OCTOBER 25, 1933

The pencil of the gods must write dully on a resisting surface.

This morning at the dawning I stood on the riverbank to pray. I knew then that the ancient ones were wise to pray for peace and beauty and not for specific gifts except fertility, which is continued life. And I saw that if one has even a small degree of the ability to take into and unto himself the peace and the beauty the gods surround him with, it is not necessary to ask for more.[6]

OCTOBER 28, 1933

Just now as I watched the ever-changing beauty, I saw a cloud pass over the earth on long grey stilts of rain. And then as I looked, I saw its shape and knew that over the Pueblo moved the Thunder Bird. With wings outspread he slowly passed, broad tail sweeping the thirsty earth. Down from his breast fell feathers of rain and out from his heart the lightning flashed its message to the people that the gods never forget. Thunder roared from his long black beak and all earth sounds were hushed. He has gone, leaving only his mark on the land, but I can still see his broad wings stretched and the white rain feathers dropping from his breast. And any fear, lingering from those childhood days when I, unafraid, was made to fear lightning, has gone. Did it not come from his heart? If it should seek me out or find me wandering in its path, would it not take me back with it? I should not mind going so much if I could look down on beauty as is earth's today.[7]

DECEMBER 2, 1933

Today there were shadows of eagle wings on the marl as I came home. Beside me A talked while all of me was conscious only of those wings that floated above the tawny hills. For the eagles are of the gods and I can feel in their presence only great awe. Sometimes it seems as though this force flowed into me most noticeably after I had given of me in some way and was depleted.

DECEMBER 22, 1933

Even in these rushed days there is such peace in between. There are moments when two eagle feathers can fill me with joy; when the last rays of the sun touch my forehead as I stand by the kitchen door; when the outline of To-tavi is marked in rhythm against a clear western sky; when even the wind is part of it all. Surely such moments do something to me. If not, it is because I hide beneath the pettiness. I have no apparent goal. I only know that I am living a day at a time as I feel the way.

FEBRUARY 22, 1934

It is strange that I who love the sun am so relaxed and filled with a peace like the calm before a storm now that clouds have greyed the sky. This wind does not irritate me—perhaps because it brings rain. The poor dry earth. There is not even a ragged bit of snow in the shadow of a cedar, and it is only February.

I had almost forgotten how to lie curled on the ground or here on my couch, content just to look and feel and enjoy the thoughts that come. Rushing with things to be done crowding, crowding is such a waste of living. There need to be hours of this.

APRIL 1, EASTER—1934

This morning as I was quiet, it came to me—what I believe. All the good, all the peace and all the beauty that make up that Force which exists, and of which we are aware through our souls.

Yesterday I went to see Chai, who surely cannot come again to my house, and the Old One was there. It is so natural as the old people sit on a low bedroll, to kneel before them so we can look at each other. It is such natural affection we have, one for the other, and no embraces mean more than theirs. I am glad he came to see Chai. They were such good friends and something so apart from that friendship should not have separated them.

MAY 25, 1934

There was a time when I sought to put out of my life or go away from those humans who irritated me or disturbed the rhythm of my being. Now that I have come this far on the way, I know that the only way is to become impervious to the irritation.
(note. 1936. I am dubious. Perhaps it is I who am out of rhythm.)

SEPTEMBER 19, 1934

This morning soon after dawn there came little clouds over the Mesa that were like the wild geese winging south—but silent geese. The other night there was a long-legged bird cloud beside the moon. Could that be where my blue heron has gone these months? The bridge arch

is not the quiet vantage point it once was. I suppose I should look with approval upon all the improvements, but I cannot. I hope they will leave one canyon road-less and still.

SEPTEMBER 23, 1934

The other morning I found that when I did not let things press too closely, I kneaded bread rhythmically and with pleasure. I realized then that it was better to send people away without food than to have the mirror of my soul clouded.

I am glad the summer is over. I cannot go through many months without these periods of quiet. It is like Oqu's reaction to the murals. I had felt it but did not know what was wrong until he said there needed to be small designs between the figured groups to mark the rhythm. I have to live that way in order to retain the balance.

SEPTEMBER 25, 1934

I cannot work. I can only sit here in the sun. Perhaps somewhere earth forces are breaking forth. Perhaps it is just I. I am very conscious of something happening. There is not a cloud in the west, a few above the valley. The aspens have turned. The wind is cold. I sit waiting. For what?

OCTOBER 17, 1934

"Are you ever frightened?" she asked me. When I asked, by what, she said, "The solitude." Without hesitation I told her, "Never, only people frighten me." That was all, but it made me think.

She had come back to this country of sunlight and shadow after months in a city. Here where mesas rise up from the river, there is only the sound of the water. Perhaps the change was too sudden, too great, and the strangeness frightened her. Perhaps she has a city soul.

Why should anyone fear solitude? I can understand fear of the elements when they set loose their fury, which man has no weapon to combat. I can understand fear of the animals that live in solitary places. But in solitude itself there is nothing that can harm one. Perhaps man's soul stands stripped in solitude, and he fears what he sees there. I feel very small and of little worth in the presence of great spaces and deep silence—but not afraid.

JANUARY 6, 1935

She said, "It may be that M. P. found peace in the ocean." But one does not seek nor find peace and happiness. It comes when one is ready for it. One prepares through the years for it and waits until the gods send it.

JANUARY 11, 1935

Rain again. The gods would not have their people come to the departing yet. The rain softens the sharp outline of the mesas. I hope when the years have sharpened my outlines in the passing, some inner glow will soften them.

JANUARY 27, 1935

It was hot in the sun today, and even now at twilight there is no coldness in the air. I found myself looking at the cottonwoods to see if buds were swelling. There is a new evening star with a small one quite near it. I cannot recall that before. Usually it is a solitary, lonely one. I am glad there are two together.

FEBRUARY 7, 1935

On grey days like this I so often think of wild geese flying south. I heard their honking one October day and went out into the gently falling rain to see the swaying black line of them against the grey sky. Soon they entered the canyon, and I watched closely, following against the dark mesa that darker line. Now above, now below the broken mesa rim they flew, with never a moment of hesitation, with always the memory of warm, plentiful feeding grounds, and an old trail to them. Where the river turns again, they rose above the mesa, and my last glimpse was that swaying line against lighter clouds— winging southward. Death could be like that.

FEBRUARY 14, 1935

Again I have known days of cloud gathering and snow flurries, wild wind-driven snow, winds that loathly retired before a calm that brought soft silent snow. That was yesterday. Today the sun shines here, but clouds hang low on the Sangre peaks and beyond Shumo. Again I have touched the fringe of the unknown and been drawn to it, not by my seeking, which is the only real way.

LETTERS

$\mathcal{M}$ost of the surviving letters of Edith Warner were written to her goddaughter, Peter.[1] The letters were rarely dated, and so I made no attempt to arrange them chronologically. I corrected archaic spellings—like *tho* and *thot*—and deleted names when necessary to protect the privacy of people, replacing them with the bracketed letter [N]. Edith used the other initials in her letters. Letters became the bulk of Edith's writing in her later years.

THURSDAY

Peter dear,

The final word has come at last and Los Alamos closes Jan. 22nd with the whole place evacuated by Feb. 8th. They are allowed to tell only those connected that it is being taken over by the army. So keep it under whatever little gadget you wear on your head.

Great trucks go up via Española and back this way—lumber I guess for buildings.

I still can't believe it and wake in the night thinking I've dreamed it. Practically the whole countryside seems leaving the mesas—and here am I. It undoubtedly means no more Stacy trucks for the army will haul its own things. So I can't count on sending in vegetables. What they might mean as far as I'm concerned, I can't know. My friend Oppenheimer stopped one day with some other scientists, but then I knew nothing. That was still investigation stage. Whether he will be there I know not. In fact, it is all very secret—the L.A.'s don't know what it is all about. I feel as though a volcano were grumbling beneath me.

Thank you for the reaction of Rafael & Juanita. I'd never have known. I saw Diegito yesterday. He'd just wakened—smiled and talked to me and let me hold him when he got up. He grows so.

We went over because Darling Diego—now Pvt J. D. M.— sent me a V. letter and asked me to explain to his mother. She had one, too, but had no idea he'd been shipped overseas. We don't know where but port is San Francisco and he said it was like summer. He was so sure he'd be kept here as instructor. He's gained 10 lb. already! Hope they put him to work.

If Nat's letter to Cady wasn't returned, it was forwarded. From Cady's not wanting to see people here I'd say he didn't want to answer. Or he may be overseas. I'll ask Dorothy McKibben, who's coming out Sunday. I seldom see anyone who knows Cady and have heard nothing about him.

Godfather has Pablo's picture against his cigar box and was pleased. He had a tooth out Monday—just chanced to find the dentist at the village—but has gotten over it. He likes to sleep late these days and slowly chop wood when it's warmer. Now he's tearing up the floor because its wobbling does things to the radio.

It is warmer today and the horse being out I'll walk for the mail.

Bettie invited us to her house for Christmas—with the

Scoutes & 4 soldiers. I confess I am relieved to have a good excuse. I'd like a few boys here but can't get them out.

Peter dear,

Godfather is mending an old pair of work gloves before going to milk and I'm waiting for Kitty [Oppenheimer] who said she'd stop for cookies on her way up to art class on the Hill. Have you heard that the man who bought the place next door to her is building a garage right in front of her picture window and she is trying to sell? She hasn't heard from Helen—is worried a bit.

We are now beginning to feel like people again after the strenuousness of the Zuni trip followed by people Friday, 16 for turkey dinner Saturday, Facundo's family and Allene for the day

Sunday, a big wash yesterday. Driving 300 miles without a stop there and back plus being up most of the night takes its toll, but it was well worth it.

You must go some time when you can do it without rushing. The first time there is so much to see and all is so new that there can't be the concentration I'd like. I want to go again and stay in one house all night. Mary Ford did that but she goes every year, this time staying over until Sunday. I think she knows a Zuni woman, which is ideal. Though we made Wallace's house headquarters and had dinner there Wed. night, we slept at the school.

Mrs. Gonzales was introduced by Bertha Dutton, Museum person who knows her well and stayed at the place in a bedroom. We had the use of the rest room, which is large and has 4 davenports, and the bathroom. To be sure we were there only 2 hours but that helped. Norris, who drove, slept longer. When I thanked Mrs. G she asked if I were not a friend of Bill Schultz and said he'd spoken of me. She was very cordial and said we always could stay there.

You have heard about the Shalako from Heinrich and read about it, so I won't try to put it on paper. When you come I'll tell you what we saw. It was so much more than I anticipated and the fact of seeing altars, hearing long prayers, being right beside a dancing figure in a mask makes me feel a little closer to kiva things here.

Now it is Thursday and I want some word to go out today. Had things to be done, people, weary—same old story.

Perhaps you can picture Corn Mountain at sunset with a new moon accompanied by a star and the western sky aglow until the last light had faded. It was with this setting that the Shalako took up their places across the river and then at dusk crossed the causeway to stand below us, tall dim figures that were not men. Then to the soft sound of bells tied to legs black-blanketed figures with white caps passed us while the tall figures kept watch beside the river. When we returned they had gone to their houses and the men who take on this manifestation of the gods sat beside the altar and their masks while together they recited a long and repetitious prayer. I think these moments of ceremony and prayer were more impressive to me than the dancing itself. Bits of the whole thing keep coming back to be recalled and thought about. I am very grateful that we could go—especially godfather. He tells it all in great detail to all the village people who come and I hold in my heart the sight of him in his chair telling Sandy on the little low chair where he could look at g.[odfather] and hear every word. When S. left he said, "Sometime I'll bring my little one to listen to Meh-meh."

Today is bread day—white and brown and cookies. I do not rush but it keeps me going. More someday soon.

Love to both,

[N] not working—same old story. Haven't seen Slim—don't believe he would go—will keep ears and eyes open.

SUNDAY NIGHT

Peter dear,

While godfather smokes a Christmas cigar and music from Manhattan (!!) comes over the air, I'll try to concentrate on a letter to you. He spent the day in the village for the Matachines dance, which was postponed by torrents of rain and a plaza of mud until today. Today was clear and cold, so he went on horseback—as he did yesterday afternoon when the children danced and Slim left.

Yes, Slim came home ten days ago—looking very seriously handsome in uniform. He has gained in weight but drill has made him hard—not fat at all. On the day he came, the children heard it and the boys in a body came to the house, shook hands with him saying How do you do, Father Slim, and lined up around the room. So Desideria told godfather. I wanted to weep.

I saw him when I came from town last week for a few minutes. Then we gave him his choice of coming for dinner with some little boys or his family. He chose the latter for Christmas day. They came about 4—the rain having stopped a bit—with Diegito and the rest. There were 9 of us and Slim besides his mother. D's first tree was the centerpiece with his gifts around it—Cream of Wheat, little cans of cereal, moccasins, 2 tiny spoons I had. After dinner, godfather told them about the Hopi trip and I hushed the child.

Again there was no chance to talk with Slim, but neither was there any strain. By that and his shaking hands twice as he said goodbye, I know he understands how I feel. He probably will be sent into action, though he didn't say so.

I haven't heard from Rafael since the letter of which I wrote you—except a Christmas card. Neither had Juanita!

Dizzie, who gave me a buffalo hunter card, and Lorenzo leave tomorrow for Fort Bliss. That finishes the list. Did I tell you Larry Green sent pictures, godfather a tie and me 2 handkerchiefs? It was pathetic and illuminating. I'm sending Vel a letter Ramos wrote, asking her to send it on to you.

My hand is worse than ever tonight—don't know why. We had our usual Christmas Eve with the little fire, candles, radio carols and mass, gifts under a small tree here in the living room—but punctured by thoughts of the boys, whose hearts were in the village or wherever home was, and of those who live in fear and hunger.

I was glad there was not the usual quantity of gifts. Godfather was pleased by the warm pajamas—and I relieved to know he'd be warm for several years. He says "Thank you, dear godchildren, for helping keep me warm." As for me—well, I can discard my ancient torn purse for my metropolis one that Vel gave me some years ago because now I have a 1942 version for my reserve best one—just in case I have to go to a city ever. Thank you, my dears.

We hope you had an enjoyable Christmas and are back at the farm happily together.

Our love to you,

Godmother

SUNDAY NIGHT

Peter dear,

Godfather says no wonder we haven't heard from you since I never write! But weeks here are the usual cycle and Sunday seems to be callin' day. Today we worked in the garden—piling up winter squashes, picking winter pears and tomatoes. Before we got parsley & thyme potted Anita & baby came, so we came to the house. When she left, the day was gone. She said she hadn't heard from you—nor had she written. Tony has been working on the house, doing some pictures—and drawing $20 weekly from the U.S. He's having a N.Y. show this fall and should be getting more pictures done. They went to Apache Feast and he'd gone piñon hunting today—perhaps with an eye to our haunts. She's wearing her hair in 2 braids and it is becoming.

Tomorrow is Taos Feast. I've asked Facundo to take godfather. I can't take it this year. I hope the clouds blow away in the night. Now it is cold. We had heavy frost a week ago and then hot weather all week. Aspens have turned and the Sangres are their most beautiful. Chamisa is golden and some cottonwoods are turning. Haven't seen geese yet but 2 white herons (smaller than the blue) fish in the little water left in the lagoon. Kitty Schlates was here a few minutes—staying on through Feb.— asked when you were coming.

There has been a silver crescent over To-tavi and Venus is above the quiet place. It is time you were here!

I do hope you've continued to gain in weight and energy. Such a silly thing to let yourself get into that state—says I who've done it again and again.

If you have even a tentative plan for coming, please tell me. I've turned down several people—happily—and now Hazel wonders what the situation is. I'd rather not have her so late for it means constant fires in the other house and we haven't gotten even enough pineknots for you.

No word from Rafael and Juanita though Santana heard— having written at my urging. I hope he's been able to keep on the wagon and that they're working well. A return now would be right back into the mess. Do they know an Englishwoman is living in their house? Marie wangled it! The woman is not in my good graces and I hate being rude to her—the only way to remain uninvolved. Faith & Aileen both have had sad experiences with her.

Discussion group meets here again tomorrow night— hoping for more interested groups.

Do eat and eat and sleep.

Much love,
Godmother

Peter dear,

NBC Symphony concert over the air; clouds and blue sky over the mesas; a cool breeze relieving the heat; godfather combing his hair after a river bath. And I slipless and hoseless!! Sunday means no alarm, a leisurely breakfast in housecoat and Time (drat it!) cleaning chicken water pans, much milk & cheese business, bed-changing—things no ordinary day has time for. Now I've watered portal plants, sorted laundry, written "5 Cents" [a nickname for a San Ildefonso boy in the military] and read a bit in "As I Remember Him." My cracked lens bothers eye work but I'm sending it off this week. Maybe later I'll pick berries. Much work for me in the garden but I can't seem to get to it. Women come down Mon. & Thurs. for vegetables and it takes all morning to gather garden fair—corn & tomatoes about to begin.

I didn't prod Ceda, I just handed her a stamp and said "Please write Peter about Slim. I haven't time." Long letter from Rafael on day after wedding anniversary—still complaining about Juanita. Think he's enroute home. Phillip Montoya and Tomacito are back. Ceda says Ramos is in Berlin. Did you hear Ed Murrow from there today?

I'd suggest investigating travel and being prepared to take off if and when an opportunity presents itself. Neither of us seems able to settle down to any serious correspondence and my time is so limited now. We work best when together anyhow. I should know by now that no human pressure avails unless the time is right, but I believe in being ready for an opening.

M. Baker [Neils Bohr] hasn't been here yet but Ellen W., who is to bring him down, thinks he'll be back.

Last Sunday evening I went up the To-tavi trail—one of those compelled times. The rocky place seemed a place to be hurried through but I found a tiny stone on the trail. Just beyond it is a fairly level place and immediately the tempo changed. It seemed such a still place—a special place—and there I lingered all week. The spirit of it has been with me.

Several times I've heard a piercing bird cry and twice I've seen this—a crow flying down the river and darting around it, down toward it and then up, a small hawk screaming defiance.

Your Kelly weekend description was enjoyed. I'm intrigued by the child—and disturbed—and by Kelly's bird and reaction to yours. What a job Helen picked for herself! I'd so like to see her and Kelly, but especially Helen.

You'd never mentioned "The Ten Grandmothers" and I was saving it for your coming, so I loaned it to the giver, but will read it someday. Virginia sent me Bill Mahwell's[?] book— just started it.

I don't see New Mexico magazine and don't know who dancers are—may be Tesuque or in background S. I. I never saw dancers wear moccasins.

Tomacita has been helping me a day a week and last week did laundry at home. She tells me drinking has increased and even pre-boarding-school kids do it—one has been drunk several times. I believe he goes to I.[ndian]S.[chool] in fall. Why the Indian Service prohibition man can't get that cantina at El Rancho is beyond me. I wonder if Evans knows. Of course they'll get it anyhow but that is so easy. [N] ([N]'s wife) goes up for it and imbibes freely. If the returning soldiers sit around and drink there is no hope. [N]'s husband [N] (ex-service) has become a drifter & a drunkard beat Louis up, etc. The California wine they get is aged electrically and acts like a drug, so a Cal. man told me. In the midst of such power they turn to liquor and betray what the gods gave them. I wake in the night all tense thinking about it—and have to cycle[?] myself untied! Damn the stuff.

I'll go to the garden I guess. Wish you were here.

Our love to you both.

GF & GM

MONDAY

Peter dear,

I am going to try this contraption of the devil for your sake.[2] My fingers clutch a scrubbing brush better than a pen these days, though what the hunt system will do to my thoughts is another matter. It has been a month I'm sure since I wrote, but there seemed no end of things to be done and when night came, I was too weary to wrangle a pen.

The honeymooners were here only 11 days, but those days were given over to food and dishes. That meant a whole box of laundry to be done and all the cleaning since their departure. They spent several days in town, more in Albuquerque and are now at home. Mary is so nice that I wonder how Ernest ever drew such a prize. She is a bit younger than I but has white hair, taller, dresses well, hair curled, makeup moderate, good figure and a real person. She has worked all her life, supports an old mother and raised a boy—worked in E's office 19 years, so knows the people he does and has much in common with him. She loved it here and almost wept at leaving. He is a much nicer person now. She is as much in love as he and is so happy she feels selfish. As Allene says—they had dinner at La Fonda with her—their very evident happiness does a body good to be near. Bettie approved, too, though I haven't seen her since.

Before they came, I'd been going in weekly for 2-hour sessions with the dentist and on the last day, had a tooth out—

dashing home to cook lunch and speed them on their way. So it has been a strenuous fall, but a very mild and beautiful one with a killing frost only last week. We picked the last raspberries Wednesday. It helped no end to have the garden while they were here.

We took them to Pajarito one Monday and had a steak. Mary had all pockets full of shards. Last Monday Godfather and I had our last fling. We found several small ruins, tramped miles over mesas and didn't bring even a stick of wood to make it utilitarian. The day was perfect—even to deer tracks. When Miss Oleman heard about it, she suggested taking the children—just what I've wanted—so I hope we can go tomorrow to Navawi. GF has gone to ask the gov., since the men are supposed to cut logs or something.

Slim is due home any day. Sandy and Pete's boy left several weeks ago—haven't heard yet. S. came over to say goodbye AND so did darling Diego. Only he was refused finally by the army and has taken some kind of course in aviation ground work. He expects to be an INSTRUCTOR!!—and not to be sent out of the country. He would. The Martinez family plays safe. Tony hasn't written me and I am so mad at him. Very soon I'm going to write for my money. When he asked for it and I said how much, his reply was It is a lot for YOU. Married men are about to be drafted at once in N.M. and I fear Facundo will have to go. Tomacita has to have some kind of treatment midway of the month and when the time was right, Dr. C. had to be away. I do hope it can be done before F. goes. Rafael sent a card last week—may get a furlough.

GF reports some of the kids played hooky and trip is off. My face hurts—haven't liked the way the socket acted—so will go in the morning to see what is up. Gosh. Had just gotten into my stride but must to bed now—head splitting. Wish you were on your way out but know your job is there.

Much love from us both,
Godmother

Peter dear,

It is a cloudy, cold windy day so no garden work. Adam & godfather plowed Monday. Soon I'll walk over for mail to try to get the kinks out of my back and cobwebs out of head.

Finished up Red Cross business yesterday—Tomacita & Juanita G. did most of work—and got money sent in. Had planned to go in today but gas is too low. So Adam took money & brought out food.

Went over Sunday to see about the money and found turtle dance with Koshare in South Plaza. Watched it for a while—no chorus or drum.

Am interested in chorus and dancers coming in your picture. Wonder about new blue one. Goll darn the miles!

Glad you liked Faris. Don't understand about A. P. council voting. Who hand picked delegates before Aberle? As far as I can learn, no meeting was held—hence no note on Brophy—just secretary an Aberle man, taking authority. S.[an] I.[ldefonso] did not attend a meeting, nor receive notice of one, never registered an opinion.

The disunity among Indians is probably no greater than among white race. The only answer I can find is education toward awareness of universal problems. I doubt if emphasis on race unity for what can be gotten out of it is wise in this age.

The I[ndian]. S[ervice]. problem might be solved by having a wise Anglo executive with a group of Indian assistants, representing the various tribes—picked as men who knew sectional needs. That might develop a man acceptable to all to take Commissioner's place.

Because of criticism Brophy may be extra careful. All we can do now is hope and keep eyes open.

Having L.A.ers 4 nights a week this month and usually 10 in a group or 2 groups. Booked up through June. Couldn't do it without the ten weeks' respite.

Godfather is mending a rug—has to stay out of wind. Must plan garden layout with him tonight and write some of the boys. Ramos wrote home after hearing of mother's death—great shock. We haven't heard from Slim since just after arrival in England.

Evan's adult educational program brings teacher into discussion group plan. I'd like to have seen it worked out as a purely pueblo thing. Not actually started yet. Will we *ever* get done talking?

Read "Solution in Asia"—Owen Lattimore—if you run across it. Power can be so many different things.

Love,
Godmother

THURSDAY

Peter dear,

A round moon sinks behind To-tavi; godfather snores gently in his bed; the Wacs have not gone to work yet though any moment their bus should pass. In a little while I'll stir up pancakes to have with some sausage—we get tired of eggs and wish the English had some of them.

I fear you do the Warners as a diminishing tribe an injustice! We *are* stubborn as any mule but we do not get angry because good friends give advice. We'd be dolts if we did. I do not say we accept the advice, but we listen without anger.

You've had my letter by now telling of plans for 2 weeks in April without L.A.ers. I am also cutting down number of nights. In fact, I tried to subtly put such words in D. C.'s mouth. You see, I'm not yet sure that it isn't all mental—though she says definitely not. I got to the point where I rebelled at working every night with no quiet suppers—G[odfather] & I—no evenings to relax and read, no time to be out save a dash for mail.

Yesterday I had more pep although that may have been getting to bed early. My neck still is sore. But now I have a legitimate excuse for refusing to serve so often and they can't be hurt by my refusing as before.

I know they are only a part of the program for me, but when they press so I lose sight of the forest. Thanks for checking on me. We all are so close to our problems that we lose perspective. It is one of the things friends are for.

Since Tomacita hasn't told you her secret, I can. Yes, a child is well on the way. June, I think. I do hope it is a boy. She asked me to take her in to see Dr. C. and we finally got to her. Condition satisfactory. She'll work a bit longer and then stop. I'm letting her have milk. Dr. C. will deliver her as she did Juanita if T. wants it at hospital. I've suggested Facundo let me keep his money for him! He was queer at first about it, then delighted she said. He's seemed more natural—and happy. I don't know what draft board will do since the order to take some farmers. He really hasn't enough units.

I got $77 for Red Cross with ours and Foster's. Tonita had a cable from Dizzy yesterday so he's arrived. I still haven't heard from Slim.

Garden's plowed, will put onion sets in soon—then peas. Nights still cold.

Did I tell you darling Diego works at L.A.!

Godfather stretching—must get breakfast—wish you were here. First chicks out of shell yesterday.

Much love,
Godmother

THURSDAY NIGHT

Peter dear,

Godfather is in the village and Tavi is howling at coyotes across the arroyo. They'll probably get the turkey I couldn't find and I'll be roundly scolded.

Your Monday's letter came today and I burned it before godfather came in. Nothing known to me happened but it may have been averted. Anita told me that [N] had Joyce screaming at

Rose's baby's christening and then he grabbed Anita's arm and hurt her. Sandy had told her how strong [N] was and how he grabbed when drunk. If a tragedy doesn't happen, it will be a miracle.

I can't recall when I last wrote so it must be long. I planned to Sunday night but Betty came out. Every night something happened and last night I was asleep at 7:30. There is more than one human can do and I'm taking on more it seems.

Last Sunday I walked up to the garden in the morning for some solace. I've never seen it lovelier—all the trees in bloom and bees by the million I'm sure. Peas were up, making green lines in the brown beds. Plums filled the air with fragrance and peaches with color.

In the afternoon godfather wanted to see the dances S. I. was doing for the priest! So off we went to Santa Cruz, found it was at the school in Española. The gym was full of [Pojoa]quecs and we stood through band music, solos, readings, announcements in Spanish—having paid 50 cents each—and finally the dancers came on. So. side did Buffalo & Eagle.

[N] & [N] were supposed to dance, but [N] was drunk. Ramos took his place. Neither he nor L. were cold sober, dancing only fair. N. S. did Belt Weaving & Kiowa. Facundo & Richard in first—good.

Very few at practice Sunday night. [N] still lying down Mon. night, [N] not there. That night godfather got tough. Next night everyone—even [N]. Monday Domicio got his 3 boys together and gave them a lecture—his working while they lay around. Next day & yesterday [N] & [N] chopping wood!

[N] has lost his job! Men not coming to work regularly are fired now. That was last week. Monday he & [N] were drinking in corral, trying to get Sam. Tues. still drunk—now planting. Either [N] will have to work or they'll get [N] to buy the liquor.

Joe says "[N]'s boy & [N] boys" are the worst though most of the boys are bad and they all go to C's house or [N]'s. Joe thinks if all were together with a strong governor something might be done. Anita thinks the boys drink in protest—want to get away from old customs. She says [N] avoids her when sober. [N] goes over to see her. She's heard he's been drunk but hasn't seen him. I've heard it, too. It begins Friday night and doesn't seem to let up for some.

South Side has Buffalo & Eagle on Sunday. North has a squash dance. Apparently godfather has charge. It hasn't been done for a long time. He isn't staying over but goes over some days to prepare. I'll watch them all for you.

I hear there is a new law enforcement man in addition to old one, who is needed at S[anta] Fe school full time! Children aren't permitted to go to town anymore. Officer came out & Domicio told him to come back Sat. or Sun.! Joe thinks D. is the stumbling block—pushed by Diego—to unity or the representative system— says they aren't called.

Faris's idea depends entirely on quality of old men—and willingness of rest to obey. But anything is better than present. I'd prefer his coming here, but am willing to meet him in town if he insists.

Ted Puck & wife Mary here this afternoon! Just married? She seems nice—liked him. They'd gone to see Marie and that they'd go up to L.A.—he knows someone there.

Tried to wear suit Sunday—must be fatter or something. Can't breathe. Shall I send it back or what? No point in its hanging here for I gave my pouf (girdle—years old and never worn) to the needy and I prefer breathing to being smartly clad. Though I couldn't see anything smart in the round ball in front!

Drat the Gallegos woman! How could you buy half a house? She may come around, if he wants to sell badly enough.

Think I've told you the news. I doubt these boys feeling an isolated unit. There are sufficient Indians out here to offset that. I doubt being able to get across successfully world need for what they are throwing aside. Not enough people really feel it. They know people are interested in seeing dances—[Pojoa]quecs at Española gave much applause & threw silver—want pictures, etc. But the majority of onlookers are only interested or curious or filling a free day.

Will try to write Sun. night—S night next week & discussion group Tues. Will have no time after Sun.

Much love,
Godmother

SUNDAY NIGHT

Peter dear,

Dear god, what a week! No wonder I jumped on Facundo last night, when with 10 L Aer's in 2 groups and Mrs. J. trying to be helpful in the kitchen, a truck & 4 [Pojoa]quecs parked in the yard. I thought F. had pushed it in. He's been playfully being tough and I couldn't rise to it. All he'd come for was to tell godfather they were having a __[?]__—the saints at their house from sundown to up with prayers all night plus food. I guess it was for Wan-Tsideh. GF was weary, so didn't go. He & Mrs. J. went over this afternoon. She says the baby has a bad cough still. Swanson says he's all right. I don't know.

Wednesday afternoon the penitentiary warden asked if I'd seen 3 Mex boys—tracks were in the yard. We'd seen a fire at 6:30 A.M.—foot of To-tavi trail—was them. That night at 11 a knock at back porch—wanted food—gave the boy a loaf of bread. We watched them go out toward bridge—got gun out.

Finally I went to bed. GF waited for several hours more. Next morning found they'd looked in windows of other house & rested on portal. Told cowpuncher trackers in morning—found tracks went across river—caught them north of Black Mesa by noon.

That day I was having 20 L.A.ers for tea—a baby shower. The truck & horse trailer had been left here, car with guards came and then back with prisoners. And me baking cakes!

I knew it wasn't only physical fatigue & nerve strain but tonight as I stood down by the corral—trees and clouds reflected in the lagoon, the mesa dark under black clouds, Truchas peaks white and golden—I was certain what was wrong. A week is too long to be rushed without a still time.

Whether I can talk with Tomacita about Ramos is uncertain. If it is right, I'll know when the time comes.

Music on the radio—old songs—of smokes—all calm & peaceful. I've had my renewal—good now. Only at noon I was still frantic inside to be done and regain equilibrium. I know how little I live on food!

Trees up the canyon, one at the tank, are in leaf. First leaves on vine at windows are out.

Haven't heard from Vel. It wasn't that I wanted to be alone with her, but that she needed to be alone. I'd rather you came in the fall when it is not so hot for walking, but will be happy whenever it is. When you decide, let me know.

I wrote Ramos that his letter made me realize how much I had been hoping subconsciously that he and Slim could bring unity to the village. It seems as important in proportion as the success of the S.F. Conference, for it seems like the one chance for peace—here and in the world. The "all" in their culture is so important that disunion is like a cancer. Their being away and anticipated return makes this a unique opportunity for demanding from the older men unity. It will be most difficult but should be placed above physical or personal services. I hadn't thought it out before.

His letter was caused by a remark in one of mine—comparing the village & the world, both torn by the greed & jealousy of men, and hoping the young men could find a solution. It made him think. He says his father's right to a certain duty was taken away from him; that he could not sit with heart & mind empty, so changed. I don't understand but Domicio must be in it. All that goes way back. I told Ramos the past was of importance only for the light it might shed on future—meaning the schism.

He was not a sgt—sometimes he writes, 7/5, which is same as corp. No one has heard from Slim. I am worried.

Must get godfather's bath ready. *Wish* I could see Eagle Dancers.

Love,
Godmother

Please return enclosed. Don't tell my family about convicts. Can have a hat made here—Ledyard McKee's helper makes em. Didn't know it until recently. So don't take time out to look.

THURSDAY NOON

Peter dear,

Dinner is on the stove and the house is in order, so I'll start this, at least, for I think I'll walk over for mail this afternoon.

Yesterday we slept late, and I milked while godfather had breakfast. Then it took until noon to get snow swept off housetops and paths made, then my arm was too tired to wield a pen.

And now the feast! I got bed made up clean and some food hot in case Heinrich came. I felt I couldn't make three trips so I'd decided not to go over for the evening of the 22nd. He did not come—nor did I see him next day.

When I got up stars were shining and there were a very few clouds in southeast. By the time I went over those clouds had spread until only in the north was there pink above blue hills. The mesa looked black behind a big tree. I parked where we did at Marie's. All was still, no wind. Then the drums began to beat and the song calling, calling. I stood against the house from which we saw them and watched the smoke begin to rise. Then I saw Adam beating the fire and the smoke formed a great gray Awanyu that made its horizontal way toward the Mesa over the valley. The hunter called, the leader called, and down from the fire came the leader, the hunter, the buffalo men and woman, the 2 other hunters. From the hill came 2 does zizaggin.[3] From the north hills base came 2 antelope running and all circled the tree with the leader scattering meal. Women waited there, and down farther by a big tree—waited to touch them and sprinkle meal upon them. Below on the road the chorus waited with deep-toned drums, and on each side of the road stood 5 dancers—men bare to the waist below which a buckskin was wrapped. On the right side of the head was a fan-like arrangement of eagle or turkey feathers, and on the left was a single black horn curved up.

I ran through to stand by Sayah's house. Suddenly the song rose strong and joyous—the animals had come—and the dancing men called out and the drums urged them on. First around the corner came blanketed women, 2 Isabel's, Desideria, Santana, Anna, who went to the center to scatter meal on the earth and

the tree. Then came the leader doing likewise and making the path to the deer house for those animals who now came dancing into the plaza between the dancing men. There at the center they danced—the buffalo strong, the women light and graceful, the deer with antlered head turning and hooves pounding the earth, the antelope running around, the hunters moving about them and dancing with them. And over them the clouds were covering the sky.

About an hour later, as I took the clouds to the arroyo, the snow began to fall. The only sounds were Topsy's bell and the river. As I stood there the only movement in earth and sky seemed those softly falling flakes. It was wonderful.

Very soon the ground was white, the mesas hidden. At no time was there any wind. By 2:30 when I went over, there were several inches of snow, but it had stopped. Later there was more—on the dancers—and that night enough to make about 6 inches of soft fluffy snow.

I sat in the truck until the drummers came out and when I looked up Adam came from deer house to kiva—so handsome in a reddish brown shirt with orange scarf, striped purplish blanket around his middle, blue cloth leggings with beaded strips and beaded moccasins.

The dance was a repetition of the morning plaza dance, save that ten girls danced with men on the sides. They wore gay Indian dresses with eagle down in their long hair. Tony danced too, wearing a wig—perhaps to disguise him. So did Anita.

The last time Teen came out with a tiny drum, and Donicio took him over to stand beside the drummers.

Wan-tsideh stayed in the deer house with godfather taking care of him while Tomacita was out dancing. The leader goes out only in the early morning. T. says W-t was so good and he told them someday he'd be a buffalo.

The other plaza had the Comanche dance with Abel as one leader. Rose was handsome in blue velvet—just a bit darker than my evening gown. Juanita Gonzales has such dignity and calm.

Pat had a good time, so did Maurice and Simona's Jose. They had shoveled a place for the dance. GF says Diego, whom he had to sit upon frequently, wanted the same but GF refused to have it done.

There were lots of Indians, the Spanish-Americans abundant as always and driving noisy cars around, a few Anglos among them, some picture taking soldiers. Several L.A. cars came down but it was a weekday, and I'm sure the weather kept a great many away.

Patrocina came up to speak to me. Her 19 year old Marine son was killed on Saipan, and she is sad. An older boy by a first husband went overseas after marrying Florence Aguilar in November—a baby born in July.

Godfather looked so worn when he finally emerged. I got him home and he never even went down to see Chico. I milked and fed animals. He went to bed before nine and slept until 9 the next morning. The same was true this morning. I milked so he could eat slowly. Now he looks rested. He came in a bit ago with a rabbit that was in his trap and now he's gone for the mail with his gun, hoping he'll see another.

He wore the Arapaho head beads. I'd suggested the bag, but he thought not. When he came home he said T. and F. both asked him why he hadn't worn it. Santana fixed his hair in a chonga and he used a woven belt, not the silver one. Both Cruz and Abel came out to touch him. Cruz came up to me when they were dancing in the plaza (morning) and said, "They came down nicely." I replied, "I am thinking of Ramos." He was in chorus on south side but stood in back. Margaret danced over there.

I've written the boys. Had a V-mail from Rafael. Jan. 5—here 22nd!

My paper whites are blooming. One [?] has a red flower, a pink geranium, and the petunias. Room is gay in sunlight.

Much love,
Godmother

I've never answered your before Christmas letter and its pic-
ture-reaction. You should have no shame about suggesting the
feeling is "revelation"—perhaps only humility together with
deep gratitude. I've been trying to find what Dr. Norris
[Bradbury] says.

Two different paths may eventually lead to the comprehen-
sion of man. The first, revelation, is a direct road, but is closed to
a great many people and independent of rational thought. Those
who can make use of it are fortunate.

I would amend it to read "of man and of the spirit."

What you and I feel certainly is everywhere but in some
parts of the earth is more shut off by the material of our culture. Eventually one feels and then knows that it is within man,
too. Revelation itself in its presentation to man is not an everyday thing. As you have learned, it can be repeated or recaptured.
Eventually it is possible, I believe, if a human being is capable,
to have its deep silent wonder permanently. I think also that it
is possible for that to be so and yet the individual lead a useful
busy life. I am thinking of Bohr. I am feeling my way here and

may not be too clear. All sorts of thoughts open up in connection with the world and its dire situation and this power so little used. Those ancient civilizations had it and lost it. It would seem almost as though too much material advance were an obstruction.

Still snowing—won't seal this until someone comes—may be snowed in—gosh, only 4 cans of milk—plenty of all else. Wed. high wind & drifting snow Mon. night—wind yesterday—bitter cold—5° below on porch this A.M.—cleaning—schools closed Al.[buquerque] & S[anta]Fe—natural gas crisis—hard on woodpile—hope warms up soon—can keep GF's room warm by constant good fire. What a winter—glad you're not coming until May.

Love,
Godmother

THURSDAY A.M.

Peter dear,

Another wet snow yesterday—all day—and the temperature zero again, so godfather is just eating his breakfast by living room stove.

When I went to feed chickens, sun shone on mesa up canyon—a bank of cloud keeping all else in shadow. Such golden brilliance those Israelites must have thought heaven would have. Everything white and crunchy again. I'm glad for the awful rotten snow and mud was the opposite of beautiful. Of course this will go likewise but I'm glad for more of it. Feast day [at San Ildefonso] was clear, warm and muddy. The dancers found dry ground with difficulty and cars and people sloshed and slid through 5 inch deep (!) mud in both plazas. [?] at tom the godfather says between toast and coffee!

I took godfather over the night before and saw from Tomacita's house, the saint processed around the village under a canopy—his path lit by pitch fires. He seemed just a doll and utterly lacking in strength or life. Is it what humans project into inanimate objects or is it that stones are alive and possess power before a human ever touches them?

Later I went to the other plaza to see the animals go to the kiva. That kiva lends itself to the scene very well and it was most spectacular. The nearness of the deer as they came from their house gave me the feeling I couldn't get later. I didn't wait to see them return for godfather was waiting.

I walked over the afternoon of feast day. Godfather was willing to drive with most of the ice melted. Coming back I drove through a river of mud & water—grateful for chains. It got worse and the postman refused to come through. I don't know whether he'll try or not.

The Comanche dance was gay and colorful with Tony and Facundo as leaders. Faces and some bodies were painted, war bonnets, beaded vests, colored banners with feathers. Chorus poor—Soltero asleep inside [N] half under. Richard, Adam, godfather [in] Peter blanket—all looking handsome—kept back crowds (most of L.A., Indians, [Pojoa]quecs). Tony played to the L.A. gallery—danced alone on top of kiva at end, came out to stand with Anita and Marie R. on top step. Pictures taken, hand clapping, etc. The L.A.'s liked the color, [Pojoa]quecs on horseback dashing and all. Since it was the Comanche, I didn't much mind—seemed fiesta.

Godfather said he wasn't very tired but showed it next day. He, too, enjoyed in his own way being recognized and spoken to by the L.A.'s.

Did I tell you I saw Jacques before Xmas? He still moans over missing you. He's opened a dancing school instead of shipbuilding or NSOing—the last thing a terrific strain because of traveling conditions. He goes in Fri. & stays until Mon. or Tues.—I didn't see him the 23rd—but really wasn't looking. I don't know how much Tony sees of him. T. has been hunting with Beverly's husband and came down with Anita to meet them in south plaza. A good contact.

Did I tell you Brownie was home for Xmas? Such poise and

he won me by saying as he said goodbye take care of my dear uncle. A letter last week repeated it. Slim's letters come addressed "E. W. & Meh Meh." No word from Rafael—no one has heard—drat him. Sandy wrote home—got his box & stone. I haven't heard. Did I tell you Diego's home on furlough?

We're waiting for Topsy to drop a calf. Wasn't sure of breeding date and didn't dry her very long ago. Awful to have no milk.

Wonder so much how things go with you, when the show begins, and all. Must get to work. Wonder if there'll be mail. Finally got boys' both top galoshes—mine are being vulcanized or whatever—from Ward's and a good thing with more snow.

Much love,
Godmother

SUNDAY

Peter dear,

Took Sam on promised picnic to Navawi—just a cold lunch. Beautiful day until late in afternoon. Got some wood, too. Godfather said he "had it in mind" to go north from deer pit and sure enough he found another dull black ceremonial knife. Then as we approached the first part of n. he called & handed me a very small quartz crystal god stone—the most beautiful stone I've ever seen. It seemed as it lay in the palm of my hand to be in tangible form what I feel. At first I thought I had to give it to Geco[?] but as I sat on the walls of that old house I knew that it was mine and that it was meant to be found by godfather and then given me. It was good to sit in that place and look out— even to the Animal Land south of Shumo. Later I wandered on down the mesa and met g[od]f[ather] near a very small rim. There I felt suddenly excited but found only an unusual piece of pottery. It seemed almost as though it were mine.

On the way home we showed Sam the drawings where your deer and eagle are.

later

Skimmed Cherokee book. The high spots seemed to be that the full bloods were conservative—old customs—and not slave owners; that marriage with whites was successful & halfbreeds not the frequent type—perhaps because of good stock on both sides. Since most of the political group were not full bloods, it has less meaning.

Chanced to hear end of G. Stein poem—a portrait of Mabel Lujan. Seen it?

Think [D. H.] Lawrence sensed the need for a ground wire when he advised baking something but for Mabel it was not the

real thing we do. Humans just aren't keyed to much of the unseen. The Phila. Group concentrated it indoors with no earth contacts. Indians won't talk about it—so g[od]f[ather] says and acts. The ritual of ceremony & dance with its exact preparation save them from too great intensity.

Have gotten my room cleaned & 3 tons of soft coal delivered. G[od]f[ather] and I found a fallen dry cottonwood near garden & cross sawed part of it on Thursday—a warm golden day. Fri. Looked like snow so put up stove.

Think—stopped & thought is gone.

Thanks for wire. We thought you across the continent & into Earle's arms. Wait eagerly for letter.

Much love.
godmother

g[od]f[ather] says we're glad you went safe—now we are here by jove—best regards to you & Pearlie. (He fell in river with 1 foot today!)

SUNDAY NIGHT

Peter dear,

At last I've been to the Valle Grande. Some of the L[os]A[lamos]ers came down for us. Took us as far as the Boyd Ranch, back up on top for a wonderful steak lunch and home by sunset. The aspens always are as beautiful as 23 years ago and there was a tightness in my throat.

The cottonwoods are green and gold with chamisa in all stages. The bath place tree is thinking yellow but still is green. This week or next I'll try to get up on our hill trip along To-tavi's side.

Geese are flying south. Last Sunday, after peach canning we went for wood. There was wind in the pines as I gathered pine-knots and enough red of lamita to make the little canyon all festive. I climbed up on the mesa to look at the Jemez—Ts'acoma standing out. When we got unloaded there were geese circling. They came down just up the river and I had to go up to see. There they were on a sandy beach—gray silent figures in the twilight.

Two gunshots down the river plus a misstep of mine sent them up again and up the river—to my great disappointment. But I'd had that brief picture.

Twice this week we've gone for wood. I got tired coaxing Facundo. It's hard on godfather though he likes to do it, but I thought once in a while would be all right. This week I have town trip and some cleaning—overnight people tomorrow—and 10 people 3 nights. By the time bread, butter, cake, a casserole, vegetables gathered & prepared are all done the day is gone.

Rafael wrote he was being discharged. Pete Jr. is enroute home, so perhaps Sandy is too.

No word from Slim, though I've written every address. Sent him a Xmas box Friday. I think he gets only surface news and he didn't get Ramos's letters, he's missed all that. So many letters from here failed to reach him, all I can see to do is to stand by ready to lend a hand when possible. I've told Juanita to have the house ready for R. But I doubt if she will. She's been working.

The teacher's gone! No new one yet.

What of your show? You've said not a word and I don't know date.

Have you given up thought of the house across the Pojoaque River? A nice woman at L.A. is looking for one as a refuge from Chicago.

Our love,
Godmother

Dear Lois [Bradbury],

After a long night's sleep, headache is gone and I feel less like a mechanical toy in need of frequent winding. I still long for a few unhurried days and you must even more than I.

Your gifts were so beautifully wrapped that I wanted to keep them unopened for a long time. We both enjoyed the Chinese wrappings and ornamentations, and I appreciated the time you'd spent on each package.

I had listed a warm nightgown when my family asked for

suggestions, and now I have *two* beautiful, warm, blue ones. They are such soft & lovely things. I can't bear to wear them and likely will continue for a while to wash out and put on the old one, while I enjoy the thought of the new.

The slip will be a joy during the busy summer when ironing never seems to get done. Now I can pass on some of the short ones—or will dresses go up soon?

You think of us so frequently and so tangibly that I never feel caught up on thanking. I do not mean to take your weekly edible gifts for granted. Nor would I have you feel you should do it because we have need or because I have shared something. No wonder you do not save!

I hope this year will have less of anguish for you, although it does not seem possible. I wish I might ease it for you.

WED. NOON

Lois dear,

You needn't have tortured yourself to write—I know how you feel and that you appreciate being here. You did *not* spoil anything for me. Things shared definitely mean more—something I still have to work on at times.

When I spoke of self discipline, I should have modified it. I

was thinking of trips to town like those you did for me, parties which your friends should realize are agony for you, coming down here for produce when it adds to tension and means hurrying afterward. Somehow you have to learn to balance those things which give you uplift or renewal against others and even those against physical drain. Perhaps most of all you'll have to face your physical self and admit it has limits. Your willpower is tremendous, but again things have to be balanced and viewed over a longer period. I speak only from experience, for I have done just that. Consequently my body is ten years older than it should be and I haven't the energy to give what I might from what is here. This is failure to a certain extent.

The wood you burned is as nothing compared with more than I can count on your side of the ledger—if we must keep them. I cannot let you do this, so you have credit.

I wish I knew yesterday's outcome. I so much hope you find relief.

Ever my love to you,
Edith

To those who made a strong foundation, a tight roof and smooth walls for a house on the side of a mesa; who endured heat blisters, sore muscles and came again; who gave brain, brawn and moral support—

Today Tilano and I ate our lunch on the "winter terrace." The hillside was white and, where the children sifted sand, a patch of snow slowly melted. But the sun shone on the adobe wall and made a warm corner for us—a secluded, quiet corner such as the bridge house can no longer offer.

As I looked at the hill and the columns of basalt, I really was seeing men hauling rocks in wagons, women putting them in a trench and mixing mud to fill the crevices. That day in May I knew I did not stand alone in this undertaking thrust upon me by events. That day there began a group project which renewed a shrinking faith in mankind. It is still too close to be fully realized. However, I would record in this way my gratitude to you as a group and as individuals. It is deep and sincere, and continuing. From the ceiling of my room, from the floor of the kitchen, from the fireplaces and the porches come memories of all you did to bring this house into being. Those memories, which I treasure, are accompanied by a current of thankfulness.

I hope you will feel that it is your house, too, and use it. The latch string is always out. We should be able to work out a practical plan for this, just as we did for a foundation that went downhill. Meanwhile I shall expect you soon for a meadow meal within the walls you helped build.

Gratefully,
Edith Warner[4]

NOVEMBER 30, 1947

I have been thinking. If the world situation is as bad as it seems, I feel strongly it should be taken to the people. The strength of this country is the people and always in a crisis they have come through. I feel though that the thing we should work for is not security as such for our own country, but peace for the world. This is not really idealistic but realistic in view of the past and the present.

I'd like to see the people presented with facts in a dignified, honest way but with a spark, a challenge. The time has passed for phrases—for freedom and such—but peace embodies freedom and security.

I think we would respond in large measure to something as vital as this is if we could be made to realize: if we had to give up something for it. We take for granted what we have and leave the future in government's hands. I'd like to have mothers, as you, and trained reporters like Ed Murrow saying what they wanted and how they thought we could work toward it. It seems to me that a country aroused would do more to offset danger of war than all the weapons imaginable . . .

My love to you,
Edith[5]

APPENDIX

In the Shadow of Los Alamos

OUTLINE

I—ESTABLISHMENT OF HOUSE AT OTOWI BRIDGE—(1928–1930)
A period when the world seemed to me a small circle
enclosing the Pueblo of San Ildefonso and the house, with
Los Alamos and Santa Fe on the fringe.

Origin and location of house
Rejuvenation of house
Introduction of Indian visitors and workmen
Description of San Ildefonso
Beginnings of business
Tearoom, gasoline, pottery bought from Indians
First house guest
Pueblo contacts—social and business

Christmas party for Pueblo
Increase of tearoom business
Bedroom used for paying house guests
Growing friendship with Tilano and Juan Estevan
Indian girls as helpers
Repeated requests leading to plan for guest house

2—EXPANSION—(1930–1936)

A period when the circle was widened by people who came to the house and the tempo of daily life increased.

Building guest house—a long slow process by Indians
Parents' visit
First guest—beginning of long friendship
Tilano becomes part of household
Lupita's wedding in Pueblo
Garden is begun—Tilano suggests using land planted by his father years before
Coming of little boys, Tilano's great-nephews, to help him in garden
Stable and corral built by Tilano for his horses and cow
Juan Estevan's illness and death
New house guests
House guest's wedding—the beginning of a relationship which greatly affected house

3—DEVELOPMENT—(1936–1940)

A period when the circle is further widened by people and a radio, when tempo decreases and awareness of intangible increases.

Tilano's illness
Head-dress and moccasin making by Tilano
Peter's annual visits—beginning of relationship which had influence on house
Pueblo wedding of Tomacita and Facundo, which caused Rafael's spending winter in household

Death of Sayah
Addition of adobe dining room

4—Transition—(1940–1948)
A period when the circle became world-wide for Pueblo and house and boundaries changed.

Draft reaches into Pueblo
Spring floods change course of river and house site is threatened
Railroad abandoned and track torn up
Pearl Harbor and boys go to camp from Pueblo
Los Alamos taken over by government
House plays part in lives of people at Los Alamos
Pueblo boys in Europe and Pacific—Slim wounded
Trinity, Hiroshima, end of war followed by changes at
        Los Alamos
Return of soldiers to Pueblo
Threat to house by new bridge—decision made to move
Building new house
Final days in old house

Joan's Cookbook

Joan's Cookbook Courtesy of Joan Mark Neary.

Chocolate Cake

(Otomi Bridge)

Melt over hot water { 1½ oz. chocolate
{ 3 T. butter

Pour over — 1 cup sugar

Add { 1 cup sifted flour
sifted 3 times { ½ t. salt
{ 2 t. baking powder
or
1 t. double action ..

Add — ½ cup milk

Beat 2 minutes with
rotary egg-beater

Add — 3 unbeaten eggs

Beat 2 minutes

Pour into greased & floured pan – pref-
erably loaf pan – .

Bake in slow oven, gradually
raising heat to 300°, for 1 hour
or until done.

Shallow pan requires shorter period

Chocolate Frosting

Sift into bowl

{ 1 1/4 cup powdered
       sugar
  2 heaping T. cocoa
  pinch salt

Melt and pour over above   2 T. butter
Add   hot coffee
until consistency for spreading

Spicy Gingerbread

(Stone Bridge)

Combine and beat well
- 3/4 cup molasses
- 3/4 cup brown sugar
- 3/4 melted fat
- 2 eggs beaten

Add
Sift 3 times and add
gradually beating
each time
- 2 1/2 cups sifted flour
- 1/2 t. salt
- 2 t. soda
- 1/2 t. baking powder
- 1/2 t. cloves nutmeg
- 1 1/2 t. cinnamon

Add slowly
- 1 cup boiling water

Pour into large shallow greased pan
Bake in slow oven gradually in-
creasing heat to 275° or 300° about
1/2 hour - test with tooth pick

Oatmeal Bread

(Otowi Bridge)

Pour   4½ cups boiling water

over   3 cups regular oatmeal

Cool   { 4 T. lard

           { 6 t. salt

Cool to lukewarm { ¼ cup molasses

Prepare as directed   2 envelopes yeast
and add to above

Stir well and add { ½ cup corn meal

Vary to taste - more or { ½ cup rye flour

less may be used { ½ cup wheat cereal or flour

Stir in white flour until consistency
to knead, Knead using flour until
dough does not stick to hands.
Let rise until double and knead down.
Let rise again and put in two pans.
Let rise - not quite double
Bake in moderate oven about 1 hour.
Test by smoothing bottom of loaf.

Page from the Warner Family Bible

Family Record.
Births.

Charles Pierce Warner,
Sep 21th 1864.   Phila

Ida F. Mayer,
Nov 19th 1866   Reading

Paul Mayer Warner,
Nov. 6th 1891.   Phila.

Edith Mayer Warner
August 22 – 1893.
Phila

Florence Haley Warner
Dec. 3 – 1899
Phila.

Elizabeth Laurens Warner
June 5 – 1901
Phila

Velma Morven Warner
Dec. 5 – 1902.
Lock Haven

Mary Hörg Warner
Dec. 12 – 1907
Pottstown Pa

LIST OF ILLUSTRATIONS

NOTES

Abbreviations

EI	Quote from editor's interview
EW	Edith Warner
FW	Frank Waters
HOB	Peggy Pond Church, *The House at Otowi Bridge: The Story of Edith Warner and Los Alamos*
JRO	J. Robert Oppenheimer
LAHS	Los Alamos Historical Society
LARS	Los Alamos Ranch School
LASL	Los Alamos Scientific Laboratory, now Los Alamos National Laboratory
MIT	Massachusetts Institute of Technology
NMSRA	New Mexico State Records and Archives
PM	Peter Miller
PPC	Peggy Pond Church
UNM	University of New Mexico
VW	Velma Warner
WPA	Works Progress Administration

Most of the quotes in the text were taken from correspondence to Peggy Church and are from Box 1 of her collection (MSS 359 SC) at the Center for Southwest Research at the University of New Mexico's Zimmerman Library. Letters to Frank Waters are from his collection at the same facility. Very few letters are dated. The WPA files are in the NMSRA in Santa Fe, and much of the anthropologic, geographic, and historic information in this book came from that collection. I sometimes used short titles in citing works in the notes. See the bibliography for full reference information.

Preface

1. Peggy Pond Church, *The House at Otowi Bridge: The Story of Edith Warner and Los Alamos* (Albuquerque: University of New Mexico Press, 1959) (hereafter cited as *HOB*), 5.
2. *The Santa Fe New Mexican* (October 9, 1977), B-1.
3. *WPA Guide to 1930s New Mexico* (University of Arizona, 1989), 277.
4. Ibid., 279.
5. *Space* (1934), notes on authors.
6. Bernice Brode, "Tales of Los Alamos: Chapter VIII—Miss Edith Warner," (*Los Alamos Scientific Laboratory Community News,* August 25, 1960), 8.

Introduction

1. Letter, Velma Warner (VW) to Peggy Pond Church (PPC).
2. Letters, Peter Miller (PM) to PPC.
3. Winifred Fisher quote taken from a letter, VW to PPC.
4. Letters, PM to PPC.
5. Alexander Blackburn, *Writers Forum,* vol. 11 (fall 1985), 211.
6. Ibid.
7. Lawrence Clark Powell, "Personalities of the West: Frank Waters," *Westways* (January 1974), 70.
8. Frank Waters, *The Woman at Otowi Crossing* (Chicago: Swallow Press, 1966), 83.
9. Letter, PM to Frank Waters (FW).
10. Alexander Blackburn, *Writers Forum,* vol. 11 (fall 1985), 214.
11. David King Dunaway and Sara L. Spurgeon, eds., *Writing the Southwest* (New York: Penguin, 1995), 231.
12. Letter, PM to FW.
13. Charles Adams, *Studies in Frank Waters,* vol. 18 (October 1996), 20.
14. *Writers Forum,* vol. 11 (fall 1985), 214.
15. *HOB,* 5.
16. Peggy Pond Church in *Wind's Trail: The Early Life of Mary Austin,* Shelley Armitage, ed. (Santa Fe: Museum of New Mexico Press, 1990), x.

17. PPC journal entry.
18. From PPC's chronology of *HOB* (September 21, 1955).
19. Ibid. (May 18, 1955).
20. Letter, VW to PPC.
21. Letter, VW to PPC.
22. *HOB,* acknowledgments, ix.
23. *HOB,* chronology; PPC papers.
24. Letter, PPC to FW.
25. Editor's interview (hereafter cited as EI) with Charles Adams.
26. In one of my interviews a lawsuit was mentioned—but Velma's lawyer, John Catron, told me he has no recollection of this.
27. Winifred Fisher quote taken from a letter, VW to PPC.
28. Letter, VW to PPC.

Part I: Historical Overview

THE WARNER FAMILY

1. Information from the Warner family Bible, courtesy of John Catron.
2. Letters, Velma Warner (VW) to Peggy Pond Church (PPC).
3. Letter, VW to PPC.
4. Letter, Peter Miller (PM) to PPC.
5. Letters, VW to PPC.
6. Editor's interview (EI) with Sue Smith, the youngest Warner sister Mary's daughter.
7. Information from the Warner family Bible.
8. Letters, VW to PPC.
9. Information from the Warner family Bible and EI with Sue Smith.
10. Ibid.
11. Letters, VW to PPC.
12. Letter, PM to PPC.
13. Information from the Warner family Bible.
14. EI with Sue Smith.
15. Letter, VW to PPC.
16. Letter, PM to PPC.
17. Letter, VW to PPC.
18. Letter, PM to PPC.
19. Letter, Edith Warner to Louise Gilfillian.
20. Letter, PM to PPC.
21. Letter, VW to PPC.

NEW MEXICO–ITIS

1. Letter, Peter Miller (PM) to Peggy Pond Church (PPC).
2. Diary of Adolph Bandelier. Much of the information about Bandelier National Monument is from the Works Progress

Administration (hereafter cited as WPA) files at the New Mexico State Records and Archives (hereafter cited as NMSRA).

3. PPC, "The Days Before Los Alamos," *Los Alamos Historical Society Newsletter,* vol. 15, no. 1 (March 1996), 4.

4. Letters, Velma Warner (VW) to PPC, and diary of Ann Sherman.

5. Letters, VW to PPC.

6. Editor's interview with Claire Ludlow, VW's stepdaughter-in-law, and Sue Smith, Edith's niece.

7. Letter, Constance Smithwick to PPC.

8. Ibid.

9. Letters, VW to PPC, and *The Philosophy of Health.*

LOS ALAMOS RANCH SCHOOL

1. Editor's interview with Kathleen Church. This was what the Los Alamos Ranch School (hereafter cited as LARS) staff called the road to the Hill.

2. Letter, Peter Miller (PM) to Peggy Pond Church—spelling is PM's.

3. LARS promotional literature. Most of the information about the Los Alamos Ranch School is from files at the Los Alamos Historical Society (hereafter cited as LAHS) and the Fermor Church collection at NMSRA.

4. *Harvard College Class of 1921: Twenty-fifth Anniversary Report* (Cambridge, Mass.: Harvard University Printing Office, 1946), 114.

5. Ibid.

THE CHILI LINE

1. *The Santa Fe Reporter* (October 23–29, 1996), 31.

2. Menu from Tomasita's Santa Fe Station.

3. Most Chili Line history is from the WPA files at NMSRA and the files at the LAHS.

4. Letter, Velma Warner to Peggy Pond Church.

5. John A. Gjevre, *The Chili Line: The Narrow Rail Trail to Santa Fe* (Española, N.Mex.: Las Trampas Press, 1969), ix.

6. From the outline of Edith Warner's unfinished autobiography. See Appendix.

7. Letter to editor from Harold Agnew (September 8, 1998).

PO-WOH-GE-OWEENGE (PUEBLO DE SAN ILDEFONSO)

1. Most of this information is from WPA files at NMSRA.

2. Much of the Spanish conquest history in New Mexico is from Brent Meredith's "San Ildefonso" (October 21, 1931), located in file #70 of the WPA collection at NMSRA. See the bibliography for other sources.

3. My Adventuring in New Mexico (Edith Warner [EW] photo scrapbook at the University of New Mexico [hereafter cited as UNM]).
4. *The Santa Fe Reporter* (August 28–September 3, 1996), 29.
5. EW quotes from letters to Peter Miller; see Letters.

TILANO AND EDITH
1. Editor's interview (EI) with Lois Bradbury.
2. EI with Heinrich Schultz.
3. EI with Kathleen Mark.
4. Peggy Pond Church (PPC), *HOB,* 57.
5. Letter, Peter Miller (PM) to PPC.
6. EI with Lois Bradbury.
7. EI with "Jennifer" Ruth Chapman.
8. EI with Jean Jordan.
9. EI with Sue Smith.
10. EI with Françoise Ulam.
11. EI with Ruth Chapman.
12. EI with Lois Bradbury.
13. Letter, PM to PPC.
14. Story from WPA files, NMSRA, collected by H. Brent (1935).
15. EI with Lois Bradbury.
16. EI with Françoise Ulam.
17. EI with Kathleen Mark.
18. Letter, Edith Warner to PM; see Letters.
19. Letter, PM to PPC.

PAHN-SHADIS
1. Letter, Peter Miller (PM) to Peggy Pond Church (PPC).
2. Editor's interview with Heinrich Schultz.
3. Letter, PM to PPC.
4. From *Standing By and Making Do: Women of Wartime Los Alamos,* Jane Wilson and Charlotte Serber, eds. (Los Alamos: LAHS Press, 1988), 129.

THE HILL
1. Letter, J. Robert Oppenheimer (JRO) to Peggy Pond Church (PPC).
2. Richard Rhodes, *The Making of the Atomic Bomb* (New York: Simon & Schuster, 1986), 451.
3. Letter, JRO to PPC.
4. Quoted from *Standing By and Making Do,* 112.
5. Mekita, *New Mexico Magazine* (April 1975), 32.
6. Letter, JRO to PPC.

WAR WORK

1. Bernice Brode, "Miss Edith Warner," in *Tales of Los Alamos,* 8.
2. Harold Agnew quotes from letter to editor, September 8, 1998.
3. Letter, Peter Miller (PM) to Peggy Pond Church (PPC).
4. Harold Agnew, letter to editor.
5. Editor's interview (EI) with Harold Agnew.
6. Bernice Brode, "Tales of Los Alamos," 8, and EI with Lois Bradbury.
7. Jean Bacher quote from *Standing By and Making Do,* 113.
8. Hugh Church quote in *The Los Alamos Monitor* (July 26, 1992).
9. EI with Lois Bradbury.
10. EI with Joan Mark Neary. See Appendix for the true chocolate cake recipe.
11. Letter, David Hawkins, project historian, to PPC.
12. Edith Warner (EW) quote, Bernice Brode, "Tales of Los Alamos," 8.
13. EI with Lois Bradbury.
14. EI with Kay Manley.
15. Letter, David Hawkins to PPC.
16. Letter, Philip Morrison to EW, December 30, 1945.
17. Letter, David Hawkins to PPC.
18. Letter, PM to PPC.
19. Letter, Niels Bohr to Velma Warner.
20. EI with Lois Bradbury.

THE GADGET

1. See letter of J. Robert Oppenheimer to General Groves in *Robert Oppenheimer: Letters and Recollections,* Charles Weiner and Alice Kimball Smith, eds. (Cambridge, Mass.: Harvard University Press, 1980), 290. The history of the Trinity test and the use of atomic bombs has been told in many genres—see the bibliography for my sources. One of the best books is *The Making of the Atomic Bomb,* by Richard Rhodes.

AFTERMATH

1. Bernice Brode, "Tales of Los Alamos," 5.
2. Letters, Edith Warner to Peter Miller and editor's interview (EI) with Heinrich Schultz.
3. EI with Lois Bradbury and Bernice Brode, "Tales of Los Alamos," 5.
4. EI with Kathleen Mark.
5. Famous Oppenheimer quote from James Kunetka, *City of Fire* (Albuquerque: University of New Mexico Press, 1978), 207; David Hawkins's *Manhattan District History: Project Y, The Los Alamos Project,* vol. I (Los Alamos: Los Alamos Scientific Laboratory [hereafter cited as LASL], 1947), 294; and Rhodes, *The Making of the Atomic Bomb,* 758.

6. Quote taken from documentary "The Day After Trinity," television production by Jon Else for KTEH-TV, San Jose, Calif., 1980; also Associated Press release June 30, 1954.
7. From J. Robert Oppenheimer (JRO) speech at Massachusetts Institute of Technology (hereafter cited as MIT).
8. The title of Marjorie Bell Chambers's doctoral thesis, "Technically Sweet Los Alamos," is from this Oppenheimer quote. When I researched the origin of the quote, she told me JRO used it to describe the scientific lure of the A-bomb. See: *In the Matter of J. Robert Oppenheimer: Transcripts of Hearings* (Washington, D.C.: U.S. Government Printing Office, 1954).
9. Norris Bradbury, see "Peace and the Atomic Bomb," *Pomona College Bulletin* (February 1945).
10. EI with Bill Beyer.

THE NEW HOUSE
1. Bernice Brode, "Tales of Los Alamos," 5.
2. Ibid.
3. Letter, Peter Miller to Peggy Pond Church (PPC).
4. Letter, Velma Warner to PPC.

FLYING SOUTH
1. Letter, Edith Warner to Peter Miller (PM), and editor's interview (EI) with Lois Bradbury.
2. *Santa Fe New Mexican* obituary by William McNulty (May 6, 1951), A-3.
3. Letter, Velma Warner (VW) to Ann Sherman, Edith's friend from her stay at Frijoles in 1922.
4. Letter, dated February 21, 1969, from Mrs. C. O. Ward to Frank Waters.
5. Letter, J. Robert Oppenheimer to Peggy Pond Church (PPC).
6. EI with Lois Bradbury.
7. Letter, VW to PPC.
8. Letter, PM to PPC.
9. Letter dated April 23, 1951, from PPC to May Sarton, courtesy of Sharon Snyder, biographer of PPC.
10. EI with Lois Bradbury.
11. Bernice Brode, "Tales of Los Alamos," 6.
12. Letter dated May 8, 1951, from PPC to May Sarton, courtesy of Sharon Snyder.

OTOWI TODAY
1. Associated Press release.
2. Associated Press release by Joseph Verrengia, "The Atomic Century," from *The Santa Fe New Mexican* (February 21, 1999), F-5.

Part II: Selected Writings of Edith Warner

CHRISTMAS GREETINGS AND REPORTS TO MY FRIENDS
1. Editor's interview (EI) with Sue Smith.
2. EI with Nick King.
3. EI with Kathleen Mark.
4. EI with Joan Mark Neary; see Appendix.
5. EI with Kay Manley.
6. Postscript to Christmas Letter, Edith Warner (EW) to Ann Sherman.
7. Letter, EW to Peter Miller; see Letters.
8. Box I of Peggy Pond Church's papers at UNM.

ESSAYS
Published Essays
1. Letters, Peter Miller to Peggy Pond Church.
2. Ibid.
3. This dance description was taken from Edith's journal dated March 1934.

Unpublished Essays
1. The following text is probably more of Edith's work on her autobiography. Part of the piece is lost—I found only pages 3 through 10, in papers sent by Edith's sister Velma to Peggy Pond Church. In the part that still exists, Edith looks back to her first visit to New Mexico. The anonymous reader of this book for UNM Press suggested the title of this essay.
2. This Edith Warner note is at the bottom of "The Basket Dance" and indicates she sent this piece to a publisher for consideration: "The typing is awful and I have time only to correct spelling. I have work[ed] all afternoon steadily and part of the morning. Some I did with a pen first but I am learning to think on this [typewriter]. I have kept a copy and if you think it is worth anything, I will revise, cut out and polish. Please be very frank and let me know how clear I made it and if you think it might interest anyone else. I know the style and English are abominable in most of it but it can be polished. Edith"
3. This material was taken and reworked from journal entries dated April 24 and April 30, 1934.

JOURNALS

1. Editor's interview with Claire Ludlow, Velma Warner's (VW) step-daughter-in-law. Claire told me that Velma "cried the whole time" because she really didn't want to, but she kept her promise to Edith to burn the journal.
2. Peggy Pond Church (PPC), from *HOB,* 79.
3. Letter, VW to PPC.
4. This passage was divided and is the fifth and sixth passages, standing alone as "poems," printed in *Space* magazine.
5. This excerpt was the fourth passage published in *Space.*
6. This passage was divided and subtly edited and is the first printed in *Space.*
7. This excerpt was abbreviated and is the third passage printed in *Space.*

LETTERS

1. Most of these letters and many of Peter's photos survived a fire at Peter's farm in Pennsylvania. After the fire, what could be salvaged was put in boxes and left in a storage unit for years. While searching for Edith's journal, I found Peter in Pennsylvania, but she was in failing health and we never spoke. The letters, along with everything else that was in the shed, were about to be thrown in the trash after Peter died on October 10, 1996. I befriended Jan Funk, Peter's nurse, and asked her help in finding any correspondence. She dug through the many boxes in the storage shed that were headed to the dump. She had given up and was throwing the last box away when the bottom broke and out fell a file full of godmother letters.
2. Edith is using her typewriter with this letter.
3. *Does,* female deer; *zizaggin,* a word Edith coined for the movement of the deer.
4. This letter, part of Lois Bradbury's collection, seems to have been written to all Edith's friends in Los Alamos who helped with building the "new" house.
5. This letter was also part of Lois Bradbury's collection and seems to have been written for a broader audience.

SELECTED BIBLIOGRAPHY

Through interviews I collected much of the history described in this book. Sources for the letters quoted are given in the notes. The following list of sources is by no means complete—a vast amount of published and unpublished material exists about all aspects of this history.

Books

Bahti, Tom. *Southwestern Indian Ceremonials*. Las Vegas: KC Publications, 1970.

Bandelier, Adolph. *The Delight Makers*. New York: Dodd, Mead, and Co., 1916.

Bartimus, Tad, and Scott McCartney. *Trinity's Children: Living Along America's Nuclear Highway*. New York: Harcourt Brace Jovanovich, 1991.

Bethe, Hans. *Road from Los Alamos*. New York: American Institute of Physics, 1991.

Church, Peggy Pond. *The House at Otowi Bridge: The Story of Edith Warner and Los Alamos*. Albuquerque: University of New Mexico Press, 1959.

———. *Wind's Trail: The Early Life of Mary Austin*. Edited by Shelley Armitage. Santa Fe: Museum of New Mexico Press, 1990.

Church, Peggy Pond, and Fermor Church. *When Los Alamos Was a Ranch School*. Los Alamos: Los Alamos Historical Society Press, 1974.

Dunaway, David King, and Sara L. Spurgeon, eds. *Writing the Southwest*. New York: Plume, 1995.

Dyson, Freeman. *Disturbing the Universe*. New York: Harper & Row, 1979.

Fergusson, Erna. *Dancing Gods: Indian Ceremonials of New Mexico and Arizona*. Albuquerque: University of New Mexico Press, 1966.

Fermi, Laura. *Atoms in the Family: My Life with Enrico Fermi*. Chicago: University of Chicago Press, 1954.

Gjevre, John A. *The Chili Line: The Narrow Rail Trail to Santa Fe*. Española, N.Mex.: Las Trampas Press, 1969. 3d ed., 1984.

Goodchild, Peter. *J. Robert Oppenheimer: Shatterer of Worlds*. Boston: Houghton Mifflin, 1981.

Groves, Leslie. *Now It Can Be Told: The Story of the Manhattan Project*. New York: Harper and Brothers, 1962.

Gutiérrez, Ramón A. *When Jesus Came, the Corn Mothers Went Away: Marriage, Sexuality, and Power in New Mexico, 1500–1846*. Stanford: Stanford University Press, 1991.

Hawkins, David. *Manhattan District History: Project Y, The Los Alamos Project*. Vol. I. Los Alamos: Los Alamos Scientific Laboratory, 1961.

Hewett, Edgar Lee. *Ancient Life in the American Southwest*. Indianapolis: Bobbs-Merrill Co., 1930.

Horgan, Paul. *The Centuries of Santa Fe*. Santa Fe: William Gannon, 1976. Originally published by E. P. Dutton & Co., 1956.

Houlihan, Patrick T., and Betsy E. *Lummis in the Pueblos*. Flagstaff, Ariz.: Northland Press, 1986.

Jette, Eleanor. *Inside Box 1663*. Los Alamos: Los Alamos Historical Society Press, 1977.

Johnson, George. *Fire in the Mind*. New York: Knopf, 1996.

Julyan, Robert. *The Place Names of New Mexico*. Albuquerque: University of New Mexico Press, 1996.

Jungk, Robert. *Brighter Than a Thousand Suns: A Personal History of the Atomic Scientists*. New York: Harcourt Brace, 1958.

Kunetka, James. *City of Fire: Los Alamos and the Atomic Age*. Rev. ed. Albuquerque: University of New Mexico Press, 1979.

La Farge, Oliver. *A Pictorial History of the American Indian*. New York: Crown, 1956.

Lamont, Lansing. *Day of Trinity*. New York: Atheneum, 1965.

Laurence, William L. *Dawn Over Zero: The Story of the Atomic Bomb*. New York: Knopf, 1946.

Los Alamos: Beginning of an Era, 1943–1945. Los Alamos: Los Alamos Scientific Laboratory, 1960.

Lyon, Fern, and Jacob Evans, eds. *Los Alamos: The First Forty Years*. Los Alamos: Los Alamos Historical Society Press, 1984.

Ortiz, Alfonso, ed. *New Perspectives on the Pueblos.* Albuquerque: University of New Mexico Press, 1972.

Rhodes, Richard. *The Making of the Atomic Bomb.* New York: Simon & Schuster, 1986.

Riley, Carroll L., and Charles H. Lange, eds. *The Southwestern Journals of Adolph Bandelier, 1880–1882, 1883–1884, 1885–1888, 1889–1892.* Albuquerque: University of New Mexico Press, 1966–1984.

Sando, Joe S. *The Pueblo Indians.* San Francisco: Indian Historian Press, 1976.

Schaafsma, Polly, ed. *Kachinas in the Pueblo World.* Albuquerque: University of New Mexico Press, 1994.

Sweet, Jill D. *Dances of the Tewa Pueblo Indians: Expressions of New Life.* Santa Fe: School of American Research Press, 1985.

Szasz, Ferenc. *The Day the Sun Rose Twice: The Story of the Trinity Site Nuclear Explosion, July 16, 1945.* Albuquerque: University of New Mexico Press, 1984.

Ulam, Stan M. *Adventures of a Mathematician.* New York: Scribner, 1976.

Voute, J. Peter. *Stranger in New Mexico: A Doctor's Journey, 1951–1986.* Albuquerque: University of New Mexico Press, 1987.

Walker, Samuel J. *Prompt and Utter Destruction: Truman and the Use of Atomic Bombs Against Japan.* Chapel Hill: University of North Carolina Press, 1997.

Waters, Frank. *Masked Gods.* Albuquerque: University of New Mexico Press, 1950.

———. *Book of the Hopi.* New York: Viking Press, 1963.

———. *The Woman at Otowi Crossing.* Denver: A. Swallow, 1966.

Weiner, Charles, and Alice Kimball Smith, eds. *Robert Oppenheimer: Letters and Recollections.* Cambridge, Mass.: Harvard University Press, 1980.

Whitman, William. *The Pueblo Indians of San Ildefonso.* New York: Columbia University Press, 1947.

Wilson, Jane, and Charlotte Serber, eds. *Standing By and Making Do: Women of Wartime Los Alamos.* Los Alamos: Los Alamos Historical Society Press, 1988.

WPA Guide to 1930s New Mexico. Tucson, Ariz.: University of Arizona Press, 1989. First published as *New Mexico: A Guide to the Colorful State,* by the WPA in 1940.

Magazines, Journals, Newsletters, and Newspapers

Adams, Charles. *Studies in Frank Waters,* vols. 15 and 18, 1993, 1996.

Bainbridge, Kenneth. "A Foul and Awesome Display." *Bulletin of the Atomic Scientists,* May 1975.

Bayless, George Donaho. "One Man's Visit to Trinity Site." *Salsa* (insert to Española *Rio Grande Sun*), December 1996.

Blackburn, Alexander. "Alexander Blackburn On: *The Woman at Otowi Crossing*." *Writers' Forum,* vol. 11, fall 1985.

Bradbury, Norris. "Peace and the Atomic Bomb." *Pomona College Bulletin,* February 1945.

Brode, Bernice. "Tales of Los Alamos." *Los Alamos Scientific Laboratory Community News,* June–August 1960.

Church, Peggy Pond. "The Days Before Los Alamos." *Los Alamos Historical Society Newsletter,* vol. 15, no. 1, March 1996.

Cosby, Gordon. "San Ildefonso." *Southwestern Lore,* vol. 1, December 1935, 3–5.

Fergusson, Erna. "Paradox of the Pueblo Veteran." *The Southwest Review,* vol. 31, no. 3, 1946.

Groves, Leslie. "The Atom General Answers His Critics." *The Saturday Evening Post,* 19 May 1948.

Harrington, J. P. "Old Indian Geographical Names Around Santa Fe, New Mexico." *American Anthropologist,* vol. 22, no. 4, October–December 1920.

Harvard College Class of 1921: Twenty-fifth Anniversary Report. Cambridge, Mass.: Harvard University Printing Office, 1946.

In the Matter of J. Robert Oppenheimer: Transcripts of Hearings. Washington, D.C.: U.S. Government Printing Office, 1954.

Kirby, Denanna. "Winds of War Displaced Churches." *The Los Alamos Monitor,* 26 July 1992.

"Little Boy & Fat Man," *Time,* December 19, 1960.

McNulty, William. "Edith Warner Dies; 'A' Names Her Pals." *The Santa Fe New Mexican,* 6 May 1951.

Meredith, Brent. "San Ildefonso." In file #70 of the WPA collection at New Mexico State Records and Archives, October 21, 1931.

Miller, Byron S. "A Law Is Passed—The Atomic Energy Act of 1946." *University of Chicago Law Review,* vol. 15, no. 4, summer 1948.

Poore, Anne. "Legends Surround the Bridge at Otowi." *The Santa Fe New Mexican,* 8 October 1972.

Powell, Lawrence Clark. "Personalities of the West: Frank Waters." *Westways,* January 1974.

Simmons, Marc. "Traildust: Marriott and Martinez." *The Santa Fe Reporter,* 28 August 1996.

———. "Traildust: The Little Lines." *The Santa Fe Reporter,* 23 October 1996.

29th Annual Report of the Bureau of American Ethnology. Washington, D.C.: U.S. Government Printing Office, 1916.

Verrengia, Joseph. "The Atomic Century." Associated Press release printed in *The Santa Fe New Mexican,* 21 February 1999, sec. F, 4–5.

Warner, Edith. "Relaxing for Health." *Philosophy of Health*, June 1925, 100–104.

———. "The Blazed Trail." Ibid., August 1925, 222–24.

———. "A Closed Door." Ibid., December 1925, 487–90.

———. "Narrow Gauge Meals." Ibid., May 1926, 11–15.

———. "Getting Back." Ibid., November 1926, 477–81.

———. "My Neighbors, the Pueblo Indians." *Neighborhood, A Settlement Quarterly,* June 1931, 88–95.

———. "Earth Feeling." *Space,* September 1934, 51–52.

———. "Pencil of the Gods." Ibid., 52.

———. "Christmas Eve in an Indian Pueblo." *New Mexico Sentinel,* 22 December 1937, 6–7.

Film and Video

"The Day After Trinity." Television production by Jon Else for KTEH-TV, San Jose, Calif., 1981.

"Denver & Rio Grande Chile Club 1939." Available on video at New Mexico State Library, Santa Fe, N.Mex.

Fat Man and Little Boy. Directed by Roland Joffe, 1989.

"The Last Run of the Chili Line." Available on video at the New Mexico State Library, Santa Fe, N.Mex.

"Los Alamos: The Beginning." Mario Balibrera, Tom McCarthy, et al., directors. Available on video at New Mexico State Library, Santa Fe, N.Mex., 1982.

Two Flags West. Directed by Robert Wise, 1950.

World Wide Web

Blast from the Past, http://www.ralphmag.org/briefsM.html

Children of the Manhattan Project, http://home.att.net/~cotmp/

The Doge's Reviews, http://www.inlink.com/~thedoge/otowi.html

Frank Waters, http://web.nmsu.edu/~tomlynch/swlit.waters.html

Gutiérrez de Humaña, Antonio, *The Handbook of Texas Online,* http://www.tsha.utexas.edu/handbook/online/articles/view/GG/fgu28.html

Inventory of the A. Sherman papers on Edith Warner, 1923–1951, http://elibrary.unm.edu/oanm/NmU/nmu1%23mss359sc/nmu1%23mss359sc_m4.html

A Literary History of the American West—Frank Waters, http://www.tcu.edu/depts/prs/amwest/html/wl0935.html

Peggy Pond Church, www.ralphmag.org/briefsM.html

Poet of the Month, http://members.aol.com/poetrynet/month/archive/canaday/index.html